Seasons in the Sun

Sports and American Culture Series
Bruce Clayton, Editor

Seasons
in *the* Sun

The Story of Big League
Baseball in Missouri

Roger D. Launius

University of Missouri Press · Columbia and London

Library of Congress Cataloging-in-Publication Data

Launius, Roger D.
  Seasons in the sun : the story of big league baseball in Missouri / Roger D. Launius.
     p. cm.
  Includes bibliographical references and index.
  ISBN 0-8262-1392-8 (alk. paper)
     1. Baseball—Missouri—History. I. Title.
GV863.M8 L38 2002
796.357'09778—dc21   2002017950

Designer: Kristie Lee
Typesetter: Bookcomp, Inc.
Printer and binder: Thomson Shore, Inc.
Typefaces: Minion and Impact

For
Chad, Trey, Blake, and Ryan

Contents

Preface

When I first announced that I wanted to write a book about the history of major-league baseball in Missouri, several of my friends and colleagues immediately questioned why I should wish to undertake research and writing on a topic that relates to American leisure. I have been laboring in political and religious history for several years, both of which are viewed as topics significant to understanding Americans. But baseball has not been taken seriously by many as a means of understanding American society. Indeed, some probably questioned my sanity. Others wondered if I, now firmly in middle age, was seeking to reclaim my youth. Those questions may be valid, and certainly there was a time when I dreamed of pitching for the St. Louis Cardinals, though I knew I had none of the skills that could make that dream a reality. As a boy, like many others all over this land, I pretended that I was Bob Gibson on the mound in the bottom of the ninth in the seventh game of the World Series. Those recollections motivated me as much as anything to undertake this book.

Let's face it, I love baseball. I was brought up with it, and I embraced it as something to play or watch at every opportunity. The evolution of the sport also captured my attention early on and continually draws me, a historian, back to the diamonds where players long since gone performed their wizardry. In Missouri, this includes the gentle ghosts of young men wearing the uniforms of Athletics, Browns, Cardinals, Maroons, Monarchs, Royals, Stars, and Unions, haunting us across more than a century. These specters are not at all ghoulish, but rather reminders of pleasant times in a simpler past that tug at us and ask us to come out and play.

Baseball is not about saving lives and making the world a better place. But life as a whole cannot always be about those things. Instead, baseball is a diversion from the more serious aspects of life, an opportunity to return to earlier times and less complex situations. For many, it boils everything down to its essential ingredients. It is a game with rules, the same rules for both sides, with an opportunity for all to succeed solely on the basis of merit. It may well be that the problems of Major League Baseball in the last several decades have resulted from the incursion of the complex, irrational, mundane existence of everyday life into the pristine simplicity of the game as displayed on the field.

At the same time that baseball should not be confused with the harsh realities of everyday existence, it is important to understand that its history tells Americans much about themselves. For the purposes of this book, I would suggest baseball's history in Missouri helps also to say something about the state and the people who reside in it. There does seem to be a style of major-league baseball that is unique to Missouri. For example, I can no easier conceive of Babe Ruth as a member of the Cardinals than I could picture Stan Musial in a Yankees uniform. Ruth would have hated St. Louis. It would have been too slow, staid, and traditional for his tastes. Musial would have been equally ill at ease in New York. Their personalities fit their teams, and their teams reflected the cultures of the regions in which they resided.

Both the Cardinals and the Royals, the current major-league franchises in the state, are in ways both subtle and complex the embodiment of the American heartland. They represent Middle America—simplicity, rusticity, small towns, Christian beliefs, and hard-working commoners—and the fact that they have won against the representatives of the big cities, especially the New York Yankees, places them in good stead with their fans.

Their best players have personified those perceived virtues as well. Dizzy Dean, the star pitcher of the "Gashouse Gang" Cardinals in the 1930s, was a southern hick who beat the best anyone else had to offer. Is it any wonder that once his playing days were over he could prosper as a broadcaster for the Cardinals' cross-town rivals, the Browns, selling homespun humor and hardcore American values? The greatest Cardinal of all, Stan Musial, demonstrated more than anyone those simple virtues. From the backhills of Pennsylvania's mining country, Musial strode across the National League for more than twenty years as a giant, but one who never forgot that hard work, good manners, and honorable actions brought him to greatness. His streak of 895 consecutive games played, the National League record until Billy Williams of the Cubs broke it in 1970, was a feat that Musial especially prized, for it demonstrated his commitment to working-class values. The same virtues also apply to the greatest Kansas City Royal, George Brett.

As a reflection of the culture that they serve, the major-league baseball teams in St. Louis and Kansas City provide an interesting avenue for exploring the manner in which Missourians spent their leisure time during the late nineteenth and entire twentieth centuries. *Seasons in the Sun* offers an account of the teams, pennant races, trials, and triumphs of the eight different major-league teams that have resided in the state at various times.

Whenever historians take on a project of historical synthesis such as this, they stand squarely on the shoulders of earlier investigators and incur many intellectual debts. I would like to acknowledge the assistance of several individuals who aided in the preparation of this overview of major-league baseball in Missouri history. Kenneth H. Winn, Missouri State Archivist, was instrumental in obtaining several of the images used in this book and in providing archival services. The staffs at the Missouri Historical Society in St. Louis, the State Historical Society of Missouri in Columbia, the Missouri Valley Room of the Kansas City Public Library, the *Sporting News,* the Negro Leagues Baseball Museum, and the National Baseball Hall of Fame at Cooperstown, New York, all assisted in pointing me toward documentary and photographic collections. Several individuals read portions of the manuscript or talked with me during its preparation, in the process helping more than they could ever know. These include Nadine Andreassen, Louise Alstork, Thomas Barthel, Tom D. Crouch, Robert Dallek, Paul Dickson, Ray Doswell, Andrew Dunar, Robert H. Ferrell, Colin Fries, Steve Garber, Jim Gates, Michael H. Gorn, Charles J. Gross, Alvin L. Hall, Tom Heitz, Robin Higham, Francis T. Hoban, Mark Kahn, W. D. Kay, Karen S. Koziara, Sylvia K. Kraemer, Howard E. McCurdy, William B. Mead, Ken Moon, John E. Naugle, Allan E. Needell, Peter Rutkoff, William Simons, Paul Staudohar, and Steve Steinberg. Several of the participants in the Cooperstown Symposium on Baseball and American Culture in 2000 also listened to and critiqued many of the ideas I offer in this book. Additionally, Joni Wilson was invaluable in tracking down all types of information from her base in Independence, Missouri, just outside of Kansas City. I also appreciate very much the assistance and support of G. Michael Green, my colleague at NASA, who spent many a lunch with me going over the points I try to make in this book. My thanks to the Kansas City Royals, Oakland Athletics, and St. Louis Cardinals baseball clubs for their assistance in preparing this work. A special thanks also goes to Bruce Clayton, who edits the Sports and American Culture Series for the University of Missouri Press. Finally, I wish to thank the fine staff at the University of Missouri Press, especially director Beverly Jarrett, Clair Willcox, Jane Lago, and John Brenner. All of these people would disagree with some of the conclusions presented here, but such is both the boon and the bane of historical inquiry.

Seasons in the Sun

Baseball Begins in Missouri

Even though professional baseball was born in New York, its roots and indeed its heart may be found in the American Midwest. And no place is more important to midwestern baseball than St. Louis, Missouri. Indeed, the first reported baseball game to be played in St. Louis took place on July 9, 1860, and the sport was routinely covered in the city's newspapers thereafter. The *Sporting News,* the self-styled bible of baseball, was founded in the city, and some of the earliest and most successful major-league teams called the "Gateway to the West" home.

In 1876, St. Louis became a charter member of the National League, and the city has never been the same since. In the years since 1876, six major-league franchises from six different major leagues have played in St. Louis. The most significant, by far, has been the St. Louis Cardinals. A franchise renowned for its excellence on the field, the Cardinals have earned more World Series championships (nine) than any other National League team. Hall of Fame players such as Stan Musial, Rogers Hornsby, Dizzy Dean, Bob Gibson, Lou Brock, Grover Cleveland "Pete" Alexander, Johnny Mize, and future Hall of Famers Mark McGwire and Ozzie Smith have all played for the Cardinals. Off the field, the team has enjoyed exceptional and sometimes erratic leadership from its founding owner Chris Von der Ahe, brewmeister August Busch Jr., and sage Branch Rickey.

But the St. Louis major-league baseball experience is not limited to the Cardinals. The city's baseball heritage also includes the excellent but short-lived Brown Stockings, the city's first entry into the National League; the Maroons of the pre-twentieth-century National League; the virtually forgotten Terriers of the Federal League in 1914–1915; the Stars (called the Giants in their initial season) of the Negro Leagues; and the Browns, who finished most of their fifty-two

American League seasons at or near the bottom of the standings. These teams, with their colorful and highly skilled players and owners, combined to make St. Louis one of the premier baseball towns in America.

Kansas City has been St. Louis's cross-state rival in virtually everything in the twentieth century, including major-league baseball. Although its baseball history is not quite as rich as that of St. Louis, it did boast one of the premier franchises of the Negro Leagues, the Kansas City Monarchs. The Monarchs were mainstays from the 1920s until 1960, when they went out of business. They were members of the Negro National League between 1920 and 1931, and won the Negro World Series in 1924 plus a host of league championships thereafter. Independent barnstormers between 1932 and 1936, they were a part of the Negro American League from 1937–1959. Other major-league teams have represented Kansas City as well. The Athletics of the American League spent an undistinguished decade in Kansas City between glory years in Philadelphia and Oakland. They departed in 1967, but in 1969 the Royals replaced them as Kansas City's American League entry. The epitome of excellent management in a small-market city, the Royals contended for the pennant within three years of their creation, then won a string of divisional championships in the late 1970s, the American League pennant in 1980, and finally a World Series championship in 1985 over the Cardinals.

These teams make up the major-league baseball experience in Missouri. It is a rich and varied history.

St. Louis and the Birth of the National League

After the first successful professional team, the Cincinnati Red Stockings, arose in 1869, baseball enthusiasts realized that there was money to be made in the game. The lessons of the Red Stockings' campaigns of 1869 and 1870 could not be ignored:

- The public would pay to watch top professional players.
- Exceptional players required exceptional compensation.
- Professional baseball teams overmatched amateur clubs, and since the pros won so handily, this reduced interest among spectators attending games.
- Professional teams could only be viable if they were located in large cities and traveled to play each other.
- The most efficient means of accomplishing these ends was the creation of a major league of professional baseball teams.

The thirty-year period from the rise of the first professional team in 1869 to the end of the century was a critical time for major-league baseball. Teams struggled to establish themselves, leagues rose and fell, and the owners and players engaged in battles over salaries, contracts, and profits (much as they still do today). Chaos reigned, but by the end of the nineteenth century major-league baseball as a business and a spectator sport had been established in a form still recognizable today.

In 1870, the first truly professional league, the National Association of Professional Baseball Players, was formed. In 1875 two teams from St. Louis participated in the league's final season. The NAPBP folded after the season, but a successor was already on the horizon. Despite earlier failures to create a major league, on February 2, 1876, at the Central Hotel in New York City, William Ambrose Hulbert of Chicago presided over a meeting to charter a new league. The National League began its first season less than two months later with eight teams. It has continued since without any break in operation, although labor disputes and national crises have resulted in the cancellation of parts of several seasons. The National League established a model of operation for all other spectator sports to follow, a legacy that has been both positive (league structure, schedule, and postseason championships) and negative (the reserve clause binding a player to his team for life, segregation of the sport, and erratic and sometimes shortsighted decision-making by the barons of baseball).

The most western of the new league's teams was in St. Louis, a city of about 330,000 residents in 1876. The Brown Stockings, owned by Charles Fowle, took the field for their first game on April 22, 1876. For context, it is important to remember how young the nation was at that time. The United States was not yet a century old, and the hundredth anniversary of the Declaration of Independence would be celebrated later that summer. George Armstrong Custer, *the* military celebrity of his era, was chasing the Sioux across the northern Great Plains; he would not suffer one of the worst military defeats in American history at the battle of the Little Bighorn until July. The Civil War had concluded barely a decade earlier, and the great military commander from that strange, sad war, Ulysses S. Grant, was completing his second term as president of the United States. The so-called Reconstruction of the American South was nearing completion, and in the next year the United States would remove the last vestiges of military government from the South. At the same time, there were important precursors of the future. In 1869 Alexander Graham Bell demonstrated the first telephone, and in that same year the transcontinental railroad had been completed. The National League itself, and St. Louis's place in it, was feasible only because of the nationwide railway system.

In 1876 the St. Louis Brown Stockings were an excellent team, winning 45 games and losing only 19, to finish in second place, six games behind the Chicago White Stockings. Pitcher George Bradley was responsible for all 45 victories, as well as all 19 of the losses. One of his wins was the National League's first no-hitter, against Hartford, Connecticut, on July 15. At the conclusion of the season, Philadelphia and New York were expelled from the league for not completing their final western trips. George Bradley joined the Chicago club for the 1877 season, and the Brown Stockings slipped to 28–32 for a fourth-place finish.

Following the 1877 season, four players from the Louisville Grays were banned from baseball for life for conspiring to lose some of their games. Its roster decimated, the Louisville club dropped out of the National League. John Lucas, the president of Brown Stockings, had planned to sign three of the expelled players for 1878. In protest over their expulsion, he withdrew the St. Louis club from the league. Thus ended the first foray into the National League by a team from St. Louis. It would be four more years before another major-league club played in the city, and almost ten before another St. Louis club competed in the National League.

Chris Von der Ahe and the Origins of the Cardinals

In 1880 business leaders reorganized the two main baseball clubs that had been playing in St. Louis during the 1870s, the short-lived Red Stockings (essentially a minor-league professional team) and the Brown Stockings. Two of the principal figures involved were Al Spink, cofounder of the *Sporting News,* and Chris Von der Ahe. Von der Ahe owned a beer garden and boardinghouse near the Grand Avenue stadium where the restructured club would play its games, and seeing that his bar business always picked up before and after baseball games were played, he understood that baseball fans would be good patrons. The mustachioed, Roman-nosed Von der Ahe soon became the prototype for the spotlight-grabbing major-league baseball team owner. He referred to himself, in the Dutch accent that betrayed his birth in an obscure Germanic province in 1851, as "der poss bresident," and the fans loved it. He spent freely, indulged his players, and built an early baseball dynasty. Von der Ahe loved the celebrity his ownership brought him, for now he was not just a prosperous businessman but a public figure as well. It was an unbeatable combination, offering the same attraction that still holds for baseball team owners.

Von der Ahe adored publicity for his baseball exploits, even going out of his way to garner it. He made every detail of running the team a media event.

Immediately after each game the departing fans could watch Von der Ahe, flanked by armed guards, trundle a wheelbarrow containing bags with the day's receipts from the team's office to the bank. When the team's new press agent, Harry B. Martin, tried to persuade Von der Ahe that the fans should really hear more about the players in the daily newspapers, the team owner responded, "Martin, you was a good press agent but [predecessor George] Munson was the best press agent. Now you make the mistake of thinking that the people wish to read about them ball players. Martin they don't. What the American people like to read is about me."

Von der Ahe would soon offer the city's baseball fans the spectacle of a superb baseball team performing in a circuslike atmosphere. Half a century before Bill Veeck, baseball owner and supposed pioneer of baseball promotions such as giveaways and fireworks, Von der Ahe had horse races, merry-go-rounds, and shoot-the-chute boat rides from a tower into an artificial lake as attractions for his games. He hired the "Silver Cornets," a marching band made up of twenty-four attractive young women, to provide music at the games. His goal was to make Sportsman's Park, where his team played, the "Coney Island of the West." He realized that he led the city's entertainment business, of which his baseball team was the centerpiece, and he meant to dominate that business.

In 1881 Von der Ahe put on the field for the first time the St. Louis Browns, an independent team that played several exhibition games against other professional clubs, including a highly popular series against the Cincinnati Reds and the Philadelphia Athletics, both National League clubs. Encouraged by the success of these games, O. P. Caylor, the leading figure behind the Reds, and Horace Phillips of Philadelphia organized representatives from St. Louis (Von der Ahe), Cincinnati, Philadelphia, New York, and several other cities for a meeting in Pittsburgh in November 1881. The result was a new major league, the American Association.

In 1882 Von der Ahe's Browns began playing in the American Association. Their home games were played in Sportsman's Park, a wooden ballpark at Grand Avenue and Dodier Street, in central St. Louis. The site itself had an illustrious history. Amateur teams had played games there as early as 1866. The first enclosed park on the site was built by August Solari in 1871 and was known as the Grand Avenue Grounds before its later title of Sportsman's Park. The Brown Stockings became the first major-league club to play there, but they would be far from the last: teams from four different major leagues would call the park at Grand and Dodier home before the St. Louis Cardinals would finally move out in 1966 and open the new Busch Stadium.

Von der Ahe's Browns dominated the American Association throughout the 1880s. After a losing season in 1882, Von der Ahe hired Ted Sullivan, a noted

The St. Louis Browns in 1884, in front of their scoreboard at old Sportsman's Park. The Browns won four straight championships between 1885 and 1888. Owner Chris Von der Ahe stands in street clothes in the center, while star first baseman–manager Charles Comiskey sits in the front row, third from left. Courtesy of the State Historical Society of Missouri, Columbia.

Charles Comiskey, later the owner of the American League's Chicago White Sox, was the best player on the St. Louis Browns teams that dominated the American Association throughout the 1880s. Starting at a measly ninety dollars a month, Comiskey eventually received a top salary of $5,000 per year. Von der Ahe thought this a small price to pay for Comiskey's services since the team earned $75,000 annually during its glory years. Baseball Hall of Fame Library, Cooperstown, New York, courtesy of the State Historical Society of Missouri, Columbia.

judge of baseball talent, to manage the team. Sullivan brought in third baseman Arlie Latham and pitcher Tony Mullane to strengthen a squad that already boasted a fine pitcher in Jumbo McGinnis (a twenty-five-game winner in 1882) and one of the game's premier first basemen in Charlie Comiskey. Although Sullivan quit before the end of his first season because of continued interference from the volatile Von der Ahe, the Browns finished second in the league in 1883, just a game behind champion Philadelphia. When Mullane left the Browns in 1884, the club slipped to fourth. But help arrived in July after Von der Ahe purchased a Bay City, Michigan, team to acquire its heavy-hitting pitcher Dave Foutz, and in September another hitting pitcher, "Parisian Bob" Caruthers, was added to the roster. All the pieces seemed to be in place by the end of the 1884 season for a serious run at the league championship the next year.

Indeed, the Browns ran away with the pennant in 1885, then won the championship each of the next three years under the leadership of manager–first baseman Comiskey, who would later become the owner of the American League's Chicago White Sox. When Comiskey first came to St. Louis from the minor-league Dubuque Rabbits, Von der Ahe paid him a measly $90 a month. Comiskey worked wonders with the team, then demanded and received top pay of $5,000 per year. Von der Ahe thought this a small price to pay for Comiskey's services, since the team made him some $75,000 a year during its glory years. In 1885, with Comiskey managing, the hitters perked up, and Caruthers and Foutz won 40 and 33 games respectively. The Browns finished the season 16 games ahead of second-place Cincinnati.

During the four-year period when the St. Louis Browns ruled the American Association, they played postseason series against the National League champions, although the term "World Series" had yet to be dreamed up. The Browns tied Chicago's White Stockings (3–3–1) in the 1885 series, then defeated them four games to two the next year for the American Association's only triumph over their National League rivals.

During this time the American Association was commonly called the "Beer and Whiskey" League because, in contrast to the National League, it allowed the sale of beer at its games. It also played games on Sunday and allowed franchises to set their own admission prices for fans. This last rule allowed teams to charge only a quarter for admission, whereas the National League had a fifty-cent minimum in place. The rule still didn't prevent the American Association from collapsing in 1891. However, four of its teams joined the National League, where they remain today—including the St. Louis franchise, which transferred in time for the 1892 season.

The St. Louis team, still known as the Browns, did not fare well in the 1890s, in part due to poor management by Von der Ahe. It was not entirely his fault,

Sportsman's Park/Busch Stadium, home of the Browns between 1902 and 1953 and the Cardinals between 1920 and 1966. Courtesy of the Missouri State Archives, Columbia.

however. The combination of poor investing and economic depression as a result of the Panic of 1893 sent his resources into a downward spiral. He began drinking excessively and that, coupled with a succession of mistresses, prompted his wife to sue for divorce. By 1898 Von der Ahe was a hollow shell of what he had been a decade earlier. The final blow, which the other owners enjoyed because of their animosity for Von der Ahe's lifestyle and showmanship, came when the league forced him to sell the club to more stable owners.

The new Browns owners, Frank and Stanley Robison, also owned the Cleveland Spiders in the National League. Until then the curious phenomenon of "syndicate baseball," in which a single group owned multiple franchises, had been limited to the East Coast. The owners of the Baltimore Orioles, the best team in the National League throughout the 1890s, had also bought an interest in the Brooklyn team. Brooklyn, which recently had joined five-borough Greater New York, was a much larger and more lucrative market than Baltimore, and the owners made the business decision to send the best Oriole players to Brooklyn where a winning team could yield larger profits. Baltimore smarted from the loss, but as a small-market city its fate seemed assured.

The same result occurred with the Cleveland and St. Louis franchises. The Robison brothers proceeded to switch the best players from Cleveland to St. Louis prior to the 1899 season, sending to St. Louis future Hall of Famers Cy Young, Jesse Burkett, and Bobby Wallace, as well as other players. At the time St. Louis was one of the five most populous U.S. cities, while Cleveland was in the second tier. The St. Louis baseball fans had a tradition of supporting the great Browns teams, and Cleveland had been lukewarm to the Spiders even when they had been competitive in the early 1890s. Why let great players such as Young and Burkett languish in Cleveland when they could go to St. Louis, where a larger population base would appreciate and support a contender?

Some decried the moves as "syndicate baseball" and charged the Robisons with creating a monopoly. Their response was, of course, "What's wrong with monopoly?" It was the epitome of big business in the nineteenth century, and the Robisons believed that baseball would become a big business. Their ambitions were every bit as great and as nefarious as those of Cornelius Vanderbilt, John D. Rockefeller, and Jay Gould. The National League sought monopoly, and its owners believed it a good thing.

With this raid on the Cleveland roster, the Spiders went an astounding 20–134 in 1899 and were shown the door out of the league. Meanwhile, to remove the bad memories of Von der Ahe's Browns, the Robisons changed the club colors by adding bright red trim and red socks.

How the team got the name "Cardinals" is open to question, but supposedly early in the 1899 season, a female fan in the stands, observing the uniforms, remarked, "Oh, what a lovely shade of cardinal." A sportswriter with the *St. Louis Republic,* William McHale, overheard the remark and began using the name in print. Although the St. Louis team was known in the national media as the Perfectos throughout 1899, they became the Cardinals in 1900. They were not yet, however, the great team that they would later become.

The Rise and Fall of the Maroons

As had happened before and would happen again, entrepreneurs emerged in 1883 to form a rival league to challenge the monopoly of those already in existence. The Union Association was formed under the leadership of Henry Lucas, member of an old St. Louis sporting family. With financial backing from a group of other investors—including two other leading St. Louis businessmen, Ellis Wainwright, owner of the Wainwright Brewery Company, and Adolphus

Busch, head of Anheuser-Busch—the new league started the 1884 season with teams in St. Louis and seven other cities.

Lucas's St. Louis Maroons were easily the best team, starting the season with a twenty-game winning streak and capturing the pennant by twenty-one games. The Union Association league itself never really took hold; three of the initial franchises did not finish the season, and a succession of clubs were unsuccessfully used to fill their slots. Legal battles with the other two major leagues and battles over players took their toll. The National League and the American Association were quick to respond to the challenge represented by the formation of the Union Association. A war of sorts, carried out in bidding for talent and in the courts, took place throughout 1884, and the Union Association collapsed at the end of the season. Lucas then transferred his club to the National League. Since an agreement between the National League and the American Association, entered into in 1883, prevented either major league from placing clubs in cities in which the other league already had a franchise, the addition of Lucas's Maroons to the National League violated league policy. Chris Von der Ahe ultimately agreed to the arrangement after a meeting with Lucas, most probably after Lucas paid some financial compensation. With Von der Ahe's permission, the Maroons joined the National League for the 1885 season. The only franchise to survive from the Union Association, they became the second club to represent St. Louis in the National League. However, the maneuvering between the National League and American Association that had occurred prior to the admission of Lucas's club weakened the alliance between the two leagues and contributed to the decline of the American Association.

While the Maroons may have been one of the strongest clubs in the country in 1884, their fortunes declined rapidly in the National League. After winning 94 games while losing only 19 in the Union Association in 1884, the club finished last in the National League in 1885 with a record of 36–72. The Maroons also were unable to compete with Von der Ahe's Browns, which had begun its string of four successive American Association pennants. After a dismal 1886 season (43–79, sixth place), the team withdrew from the National League, and in the end Lucas's foray into baseball cost him his fortune.

The American League and the Birth of the Browns

During its first two decades of existence, the National League withstood threats of competition from several newer professional leagues, including the Union Association. After all, spectators had a seemingly insatiable appetite for entertainment, and sporting events were entertainment of the first order. Money could be made in baseball, several entrepreneurs decided, so why allow the National League to go unchallenged? But in fending off these challenges, the National League weakened itself, and this, coupled with the economic depression of the 1890s and the expansion of the league to twelve teams—some of which were in small-market cities—further weakened the business.

This state of affairs prompted Byron Bancroft "Ban" Johnson, a Cincinnati journalist, and Charles Comiskey, now of Chicago, to create a new challenger, the American League, in 1901. The new league, transformed from a very successful minor league under Johnson's control, went head to head with the National League for players and for city loyalties. It placed teams in Baltimore, Washington, Philadelphia, Boston, Detroit, Chicago, Cleveland, and Milwaukee. Milwaukee as a baseball market was an anomaly, replaced the next year by St. Louis. So too was Baltimore, which soon lost its team to New York. By 1903, then, the American League was in direct competition with National League teams in Boston, Chicago, New York, Philadelphia, and St. Louis. Johnson's new league also competed for players, encouraging established stars from the National League to jump to the new teams. They were not hard to convince. The National League's monopoly held down players' salaries so all one had to do was offer more money. These star players gave the American League immediate credibility. Indeed, the American League began operations with two-thirds of its 180 players coming from the National League.

The American League's St. Louis team was one of the most storied and least able teams of all time. The Browns, named to remind the St. Louis fans of Von der Ahe's dynasty of the 1880s, would become easily the most inept team in major-league history, winning only one pennant in fifty-two years of existence and finishing above .500 only eleven times between 1902 and 1953. Yet they have engendered more nostalgia than virtually any other team other than the Boston Red Sox and the Dodgers of Brooklyn. Numerous books about the Browns' history are available to grace the shelves of any baseball researcher, and more are published every year. The reality was that in all but a handful of seasons the Browns played so badly that they gained the attraction of clowns, a little like the 1962 Mets or the terrible Dodger teams of the 1930s. Of course, anyone can love a winner, but it takes a certain masochistic love of baseball and a gluttony for punishment to embrace a perennial loser. St. Louis had one in the Browns, and while they were nearly always second fiddle to the Cardinals, the Browns had the appeal of an incorrigible but lovable screw-up. Aficionados believe to this day that the Browns were the worst team in baseball; they say it loud, and they say it proud.

If true, the team foreshadowed its perennial artlessness even before it arrived in St. Louis. In Milwaukee, where they had been known as the Brewers, the team finished last in the American League's inaugural season. The following season in St. Louis, the renamed Browns finished second, just five games behind Connie Mack's Philadelphia Athletics. In the next fifty-one seasons, however, they would finish as high as second only two other times while ending forty seasons in the lower half of the American League standings. The success of 1902 came largely because the new owners pumped money into the team. This allowed the Browns to lure from the Cardinals future Hall of Famer Jesse Burkett, and to support him with other excellent players. But the fix did not last. In 1903 they finished in sixth place, and by the end of the decade they had finished in the cellar twice, including in 1910, when they lost an impressive 107 games out of 154. Last place was a position in the standings they would come to know well thereafter.

The most impressive incident of the Browns' dismal 1910 season took place on October 9, the last day of the regular season. Throughout the summer Napoleon Lajoie of the Cleveland Indians had competed for the batting title with the Detroit Tigers' Ty Cobb, a player so driven that he alienated almost everyone he met on the diamond. Both men were essentially deadlocked throughout the season, as first one and then the other edged into first place in the batting race. Nor did this contest come down merely to bragging rights, since the Chalmers automobile company promised to give a new "touring car" to the winner. All of the players wanted that prize. Browns Manager Jack O'Connor hated Ty Cobb and was a friend of Lajoie's, so when the Indians came to town for the last games of the season, O'Connor told rookie third baseman Red Corriden to play extra deep when Lajoie batted.

In the afternoon doubleheader on October 9, Lajoie had eight hits in eight at bats, with six of the hits bunts down the third-base line. Two of the hits also looked like throwing errors on the part of the Browns, so official scorers may have been in league with O'Connor. Lajoie's eight hits served to push him past Cobb for the batting crown. Padding Lajoie's batting average did not work, however, because several media complained of the blatant help the Browns gave Lajoie and demanded an investigation. They got one from American League president Ban Johnson, who ruled that O'Connor and one of his coaches had rigged the games; the manager and his coach were banned from major-league baseball. The official statistics released by the league on November 21 showed Cobb with an average of .385 and Lajoie with .384. Cobb received his Chalmers car, but Lajoie got one as well since the company believed that the publicity value of the controversy had more than compensated them for the cost of the auto.

Lajoie went to his grave believing that he had won the 1910 batting title, with or without the help of the Browns, and later calculations of the season averages of both men determined that Lajoie was right. He had hit .383 while Cobb wound up at .382. It seems that Cobb had been credited with an additional 2-for-3 performance in a game on September 24. And that is how *Total Baseball: The Official Encyclopedia of Major League Baseball* records it in 1999. You can look it up, as baseball legend Casey Stengel used to say.

At war with the National League in 1901 and 1902, the American League held its own. It delivered an exciting brand of baseball, and because of this its attendance exceeded that of the National League by six hundred thousand fans in 1902. Unable to destroy the upstart league the way it had the Union Association and other challengers, the National League granted the American League status as a co-major league early in 1903, and the two leagues entered into an agreement to rule professional baseball together. The first thing they did was to recognize the contracts of each other's players, thereby conspiring to artificially hold down the salaries of the players by not allowing them to test the market as free agents, and then they established an elaborate system of governance. With this came a consistent scheduling system, player contract regulations, and game rules shared by both leagues. Perhaps the most noticeable product of this agreement was the advent of the World Series, pitting the champions of each league in a postseason contest. At first this was a nine-game series, but later the owners shortened it to the more familiar seven games to determine what they rather arrogantly called the World Champion of Baseball.

Beginning in 1903, the sixteen franchises—eight in each league—competed for the World Series crown. Thus the modern era of baseball began with the 1903 season, and it remained surprisingly stable until 1953, when the Braves left Boston for Milwaukee, the first of many team relocations to come. A year later the Browns would leave St. Louis and be reborn as the Baltimore Orioles, portending a fundamental transformation in the game, both for Missouri and for the nation as a whole.

The St. Louis Stars and Kansas City Monarchs: Only the Ball (and the Owner) Was White

The last two major-league teams to emerge in Missouri before the twentieth century's midpoint were the Kansas City Monarchs and the St. Louis Giants/ Stars, charter members of the Negro National League. While some would question the major-league status of this league, it should be considered top-caliber because the quality of baseball played was excellent. Had it not been for the segregation of the sport, several of the players certainly would have played in either the National or American League. Not to recognize these teams for their high quality is to continue the racist thinking that led to segregation in the first place.

James Thomas "Cool Papa" Bell, one of the greatest players of the Negro Leagues, played for both the St. Louis Stars and the Kansas City Monarchs. His reputation as the fastest man in baseball gave rise to many stories. Satchel Paige claimed that Bell could turn out the light and be in bed before the room got dark. In 1972 Bell was inducted into the National Baseball Hall of Fame. Courtesy of the Negro Leagues Baseball Museum, Kansas City.

The Monarchs were the most successful African American baseball team in American history. The Giants, who became the Stars in 1921, also played several years of championship-caliber baseball in the 1920s. The two Missouri teams even battled each other on occasion for top league honors. Both teams existed as independents before joining the nascent black league in 1920, but while the Monarchs operated until 1960, the Stars failed in 1931, although they were revived intermittently for the rest of the thirties as an operating club.

How did these great baseball teams come to be?

Although baseball was as popular among African Americans from the 1860s on as it was among whites, major-league baseball rebuffed repeated attempts by black players to enter the sport. In isolated incidences a black might play professionally in the minor leagues, but following a notorious 1887 exhibition game between the Chicago White Stockings of the National League and the Newark Eagles of the International League even that changed. The incident involved Adrian "Cap" Anson, one of the best players of his day and a legend in National League history. Anson refused to let his White Stockings take the field against the Eagles, who had two African American players, George Stovey and Fleet Walker. That winter the owners of major-league teams persuaded their minor-league owners that "the colored element" was unseemly and should not be allowed to participate in organized ball. Walker, Stovey, and the handful of other black players received notice that they would no longer have contracts. For sixty years this "gentleman's agreement"—nothing was put into writing—to prohibit integration remained inviolate, until Jackie Robinson appeared in a Brooklyn Dodgers uniform in 1947. This collusion on the part of all major-league baseball owners to ostracize some 20 percent of the American population represents the single most significant affront to decency ever engaged in by major-league baseball.

Since blacks could not join the major leagues, perhaps they could beat them at their own game, or so thought Andrew "Rube" Foster, the best African American pitcher of his era. Foster was not only a prolific and powerful pitcher but also a brilliant organizer. In 1920, out of a landscape of unstable, loosely organized black professional baseball teams, he would create the first major-league-caliber organization for African American baseball players, the National Association of Professional Baseball Clubs, commonly known as the Negro National League.

After preliminary meetings in Chicago and Detroit, Foster invited the owners of several midwestern African American teams to Kansas City for an organizational meeting at the Paseo YMCA on February 13, 1920. The Negro National League was created from teams scattered across the Midwest, with Foster himself owning the Chicago American Giants. There was a second team in Chicago, and single teams in Cincinnati, Dayton, Detroit, and Indianapolis, as well as in Kansas City and St. Louis. The league followed a no-nonsense constitution:

- Managers and owners would be fined for ungentlemanly conduct.
- A manager could not take a team off the field in the middle of a game.
- Ballplayers were to conduct themselves properly on and off the field.
- Jumping from one team to another was forbidden; each owner would honor the contracts of the other owners.
- Players who jumped their teams were to be banned from the league.
- Teams had the right to refuse to play teams not affiliated with the league.
- Owners had the right to trade or sell the services of their players.
- Borrowing players for league games was forbidden.
- Violation of league rules carried a heavy fine.
- Each owner would pay five hundred dollars to bind him to the league.

Foster became the league's president, and his status helped draw fans and provided the credibility to hold the league together despite tremendous adversity and a shaky financial situation.

What Foster achieved was nothing short of organizing a set of existing barnstorming teams into a league modeled on the white counterparts. With Kansas City and St. Louis as charter members, the Negro National League was an enormously important step in the rise of professional major-league baseball in Missouri. Foster's success was mirrored in the East when, smelling profits to be made, a group of white businessmen formed their own black league. In 1923, the Eastern Colored League arose; its teams included the Philadelphia Hilldales, Brooklyn Royal Giants, Lincoln Giants, Baltimore Black Sox, Atlantic City Bacharachs, and New York Cuban All-Stars. Soon the two leagues began to play each other in a postseason championship series, billed as the Colored World Series.

In 1920, the St. Louis Giants took the field for the first time as a Negro National League team. Not capable of competing in the league, they finished a dismal sixth place with a 25–32 record. Also incapable of competing with the Cardinals and Browns for the St. Louis sports dollar, the team folded at the end of the year. They gained a new owner and a new name, the Stars, in 1921, and returned to the field. This time, they finished fourth, with a 35–26 record. The next three years they remained in the middle of the pack, but in 1925 they won their first league championship, mirroring the successes of the white professional teams in a 1920s renaissance of championship-caliber baseball in St. Louis.

More significant, however, were the achievements of the Kansas City Monarchs, who would become perhaps the most successful team in black baseball history. Also brought into the Negro National League in 1920, the Monarchs traced their heritage to the All Nation's barnstorming baseball team put together by J. L. Wilkinson in 1912. Wilkinson, known as "Wilkie" to his friends, was the only white owner in the new league. At first distrusted by other owners because of his race, Wilkinson had a remarkable pedigree as a friend of African Americans and other minorities in the United States. Born in Perry, Iowa, in 1874, the son of the president of Algona Normal College, Wilkinson pitched on a variety of semipro teams during his early years, and then organized the All Nations team, which included blacks, whites, Cubans, Native Americans, Mexicans, and Asians. He even hired a woman, billed as "Carrie Nation," to play second base. It was an enormously successful barnstorming team, crisscrossing the Midwest and playing all comers, but it collapsed with the Selective Service draft inaugurated when the United States entered World War I in 1917. Many of the players ended up in uniform, and the All Nations team disbanded in 1918.

The Kansas City Monarchs in 1934. Standing left to right: Sam Bankhead, T. J. Young, George Giles, Turkey Sterns, Frank Duncan, Moocha Harris, Carroll Mothel, Cool Papa Bell, Newt Allen, Willie Wells, and owner J. L. Wilkinson. Kneeling, from left: Chet Brewer, Newt Joseph, Bullet Joe Rogan, and Charles Beverly. Courtesy of Special Collections, Kansas City Public Library.

Although Wilkinson wanted to become a part of Rube Foster's new league, Foster tried to prevent a white franchise owner's entrance. When alternatives failed to materialize in Kansas City, however, Foster relented and Wilkinson formed the Monarchs. It proved a happy choice. Wilkinson brought to the league excellent baseball sense, solid financial backing in Kansas City that included a stadium for home games, special commitment to high-quality play and honorable business operations, and a belief in the importance of the Negro National League as an experiment that would facilitate greater equality among the races. He convinced the other owners of his sincerity at the league's organizational meeting in 1920, being named secretary and special counselor to league president Foster.

Wilkinson owned the Monarchs for more than twenty-five years, and over time earned the respect of those associated with the Negro Leagues and with white professional baseball. He loved baseball in all its permutations, but the game also served as his principal source of income. As such, he worked hard to make the Monarchs profitable. And the Monarchs were overwhelmingly profitable in the 1920s. As a white man, perhaps, he could strike better deals with other white men for leasing stadiums and for exhibition games. But he also treated his players well. Newt Allen spent much of his career playing for the Monarchs, and he said that Wilkinson "was a considerate man; he understood; he knew people. Your face could be black as tar; he treated everyone alike." In 1928 the Monarchs paid Wilkinson a public tribute in the *Kansas City Call*, an African American newspaper:

> The best club owner in the world to work for—
>   who is familiar with the game as it is today
> who knows how to plan for the future
>   who believes in us at all times
> who stands for a fair and square deal to all
>   who gives the best and expects the best in return
> who loves and is loved by his players
>   who believes that charity begins at home
> who knows and appreciates real ability
>   who instills the fighting spirit in his club
> who practices what he preaches
>   who never turned on a friend.

Robert Sweeney, a leader in Kansas City's black community, said of the Monarchs' owner, "Wilkie stood pretty well with the Negroes. He gave employment to several Negro families. He had a good image in the Negro community—all over the country."

One of Wilkinson's more significant moves to ensure the team's acceptance by the fans of the Negro National League was to hire Quincy J. Gilmore as the Monarchs' traveling secretary. Gilmore, an African American, became the public face of the Monarchs, while Wilkinson stayed out of the spotlight as much as possible. Just the opposite of Chris Von der Ahe, who believed that his antics attracted crowds to his Browns' games, Wilkinson saw that his club's identification with the black business community would enhance ticket sales. Gilmore's wife remembered, "Mr. Wilkinson always kinda used Gilmore to make his public appearances and addresses and things for him. Whenever they had to appear in public, Mr. Gilmore would go and kinda front." It was a very effective partnership that lasted many years.

In establishing the Monarchs, Wilkinson chose as some of its core players in 1920 veterans from his All Nations team: José Mendez, John Donaldson, Bill Drake, and Frank Blukoi. He also recruited based on tips about black players from John McGraw, the manager of the New York Giants, who would have liked those players for his own team but whose club owner prohibited their signing. McGraw's tips led Wilkinson to Hall of Fame pitcher "Bullet" Joe Rogan and other players from the U.S. Army's Twenty-fifth Infantry Wreckers. That team, stationed at Fort Huachuca, Arizona, had won a succession of championships in a league sponsored by the Army. Because so many of its players came from the Wreckers, the early Monarchs were sometimes characterized as the "army team." With the help of these players, the Monarchs became a powerhouse in the Negro National League in the early 1920s.

By the early 1920s, major-league baseball had been firmly established in St. Louis and Kansas City. St. Louis had built a long major-league tradition that included a championship team, the American Association Browns of the 1880s, and continued with the American League Browns, the National League Cardinals, and the Negro National League Giants/Stars. Major-league baseball arose later in Kansas City, with the birth of the Monarchs in 1920. But the Monarchs would play just as much a part as the St. Louis teams in an era of excellence not seen elsewhere during the 1920s. All but one of Missouri's major-league teams would compete and win championships during the decade, and the other would fall just short of a pennant in 1922.

Missouri Baseball Comes of Age

By the 1920s the ebb and flow of major-league baseball teams had become something most residents of Missouri and the surrounding region had learned to expect. The 1920s, however, saw the state's teams at high tide. Even the St. Louis Browns enjoyed a series of runs at a pennant in the early 1920s before descending back into the depths of the American League. The Kansas City Monarchs and St. Louis Stars won a string of Negro National League pennants and the Monarchs took the Colored World Series in 1924. And the St. Louis Cardinals rose to prominence, winning their first championship in 1926 and a second league pennant in 1928. The Cardinals then built a dynasty in the 1930s with the legendary "Gashouse Gang," winning another three league pennants and two World Series championships. Even greater success came in the 1940s, when the Cardinals and a young Stan Musial won three titles in five years and made three consecutive appearances in the World Series.

Like the Cardinals, the Monarchs prospered in the 1930s and 1940s. In 1929 they developed a portable lighting system that allowed them to play night games when playing out of town. The result was that during the Great Depression and through World War II, with players such as Satchel Paige and Jackie Robinson, the Monarchs were among the most successful of the Negro League teams. Only the Browns failed, but even they caught lightning once, winning the American League pennant in 1944. Their World Series opponent was, of course, the Cardinals. This gave St. Louis its first and only "streetcar" World Series.

The Browns: From Doormats to Dominance and Back

The St. Louis Browns had finished last in the American League three times in their first decade and seemed well on the way to cementing their status as the worst team in the league. But in 1913 two key events took place. First, although they were again last in the American League, losing 96 games, they were not the worst major-league team in St. Louis that year. The Cardinals, who were woeful at this point in their history, were last in the National League, and they lost 99 games, three more than the Browns. The Browns at least had reason to believe they were not as bad as their cross-town rivals. Second, the owner of the Browns, a St. Louis businessman named Robert Hedges, hired a scout with the rather un-baseball-like name of Wesley Branch Rickey. Rickey soon built the Browns into winners. A few years later, he would do the same for the Cardinals.

Branch Rickey had been born in 1881 and raised on an Ohio farm. He coached and played semipro baseball and football to pay his way through Ohio Wesleyan College. A devout Methodist, Rickey kept a promise to his mother that he would not play or work on Sundays. He refused even to travel on Sunday. Of course, later in his career his teams played on Sundays, and he always called the ballpark to check on the day's receipts. He displayed throughout his life streaks of petulance, moralism, and autocracy that either infuriated or endeared him to those he encountered. He was well educated, but he listened to the siren call of professional baseball and played for a short time in the major leagues. A catcher for the New York Highlanders, later renamed the Yankees, and then for the Browns, he contracted tuberculosis and retired. He passed the bar and began practicing law, but in 1909 he returned to baseball as coach of the University of Michigan team. There he discovered left-handed first baseman George Sisler, who would become the greatest Browns player of all. In a fifteen-year career Sisler compiled a .340 lifetime batting average, batted over .400 twice, led the league in stolen bases four times, and at first base recorded 1,528 assists, a record that stood for more than sixty years.

After a short and undistinguished stint as the Browns' field manager, Rickey moved into the front office in 1915 and began to build a winning team. His process for doing so involved the establishment of what he referred to as a "farm system." It represented essentially a form of vertical integration in professional baseball, and its origination represented sheer genius. After all, what is major-league baseball if not an attraction on a playing field that draws spectators? The attraction is the players, so the objective is to place as many good players on the field as possible for as little money as possible. But where can one find proficient yet inexpensive players? The system in place prior to the development of Rickey's farm system was to find players in the minor leagues, whose team owners were glad to sell players' contracts for profit. But Rickey found their prices too high, so he decided to have the Browns purchase a few minor-league teams, stock them with promising players already under contract, and give them excellent baseball instruction. As the best players rose in the system, the Browns were able to add them to the big-league roster without putting money out of pocket to acquire their contracts. Players in the minors were referred to as being "down on the farm," hence the name for the system.

Rickey's central point in taking this approach was that since it was exceptionally difficult to predict which players would be successful in the major leagues, the best means of ensuring success was to start with a large group of potentially good players and let the cream rise to the top. A whole range of factors could arise to alter any prospect's development between the ages of eighteen and twenty-five—injury, illness, life experience, character flaws, and the like. The farm system would reveal those factors and produce, if operated properly, enough talent not only to stock the Browns but also to generate additional revenues through trades of excess players to other teams. The farm system, from Rickey's perspective, reduced the very large gamble inherent in player development and allowed the Browns to receive, rather than to pay, top dollar for the best minor-league talent.

During the years that Rickey was with the Browns, 1913–1917, he was able only to make a start at building a stable farm system, but his efforts resulted in a very good team that took the field in the early 1920s. Rickey's inability to complete what he started with the Browns resulted from a personality clash with the new owner, Philip DeCatesby Ball, who purchased the team in 1915. The Browns did not have a front office large enough to accommodate the inflated egos of both Ball and Rickey, so one had to go. Rickey went next door to the Cardinals, where he spent the next two decades establishing a full-fledged farm system and using it to turn the Cardinals into one of the best National League franchises of all time.

But even with the departure of Rickey, the Browns made history in the "roaring twenties." In 1920 the team finished in the first division for the first time since 1908. Sisler set the pace, leading the American League with a .407 batting average, driving in 122 runs, and setting the single-season record of 257 hits that still stands. He was ably assisted by outfielder Ken Williams and pitcher Urban Shocker, who won 20 games and lost 10. In 1921 the Browns finished third with the same cadre of players. This time Shocker won a league-high 27 games. It looked like 1922 would be the year of the Browns, and everyone in St. Louis was poised to take a championship.

They nearly did. In 1922 the Browns won 93 games, the most the team ever mustered in a season, but they finished one game behind the New York Yankees. Even so, it was probably the best team in Browns history. Sisler had a career year, batting a league-high .420, and Ken Williams led the league with 39 homers and 155 runs batted in. Shocker, winner of 24 games, anchored the pitching staff. The Browns ran neck-and-neck with the Yankees all summer and were in first place as late as July 22. The fans in St. Louis were jubilant, rocking the city's center with impromptu street parties and at least one riot: at a game on Labor Day, fans unable to get tickets to the day's game against the Cleveland Indians rushed the gate. Police had to restore order.

The pennant race took a turn for the worse on Saturday, September 16, 1922, when the Yankees arrived in St. Louis for a critical three-game series. At that point the Yankees led the league with 86 wins and 55 losses, while the Browns stood a half-game behind them at 86–56. Each team had twelve games left to play in the season. The three-game series, billed as the "little World Series," would quite possibly decide the pennant. The Browns and the Yankees split the first two games. In the first, Yankee ace Bob Shawkey defeated Urban Shocker 2–1. One Browns fan marred the contest by beaning Yankee center fielder Lawton "Whitey" Witt with a bottle as he chased a fly ball in the ninth inning. It knocked Witt out. Fans poured onto the playing field to check on Witt's condition, and police had to disperse the crowd before play could resume. Witt had a concussion and had to be carried off the field. Many expressed true remorse that such an incident would take place in St. Louis; one fan even exclaimed to a reporter for the *St. Louis Post-Dispatch,* "I'm through with baseball. I don't care who wins the pennant now."

That was a minority position, however. The next afternoon, with many of the thirty thousand fans in attendance forgoing church services to get to Sportsman's Park early, Browns pitcher Hubert "Shucks" Pruett defeated the Yankees 5–1. Ken Williams rose to the challenge by belting a two-run homer, his thirty-eighth of the year, providing all of the offense needed. The Yankees' only run came on a home run by Babe Ruth.

This set up a "rubber game" for Monday, September 18, and it did not disappoint, even though the Browns lost. By the seventh inning St. Louis had taken a 2–0 lead and looked to be on the verge of clinching the series. The Yankees scored in the eighth, however, making it 2–1. When the Browns' starting pitcher, Dixie Davis, got into trouble by allowing a Yankee base-runner in the ninth, the manager took him out in favor of Pruett, the previous game's winner. Pruett proceeded to load the bases before he got the hook, this time for Shocker. Shocker's confrontation with Whitey Witt, the center fielder who had been beaned two days earlier, ended with a solid single and two Yankee runs crossing the plate. The Browns were unable to score in their half of the ninth, and the game ended 3–2, with the Yankees a game and a half in the lead for the American League pennant. They managed to stay just ahead of the Browns the rest of the season, winning the pennant but losing the World Series to the New York Giants.

The 1922 season would be the high-water mark for the Browns. The next year George Sisler missed the season with an eye infection that nearly did him in and the Browns slipped to fifth in the league. When Sisler returned in 1924, the team again vied for the pennant before finishing fourth. The Browns finished third in 1925, slipped to seventh in 1926 and 1927, and then returned to third in 1928. Thereafter, the team began a collapse that lasted until their lone pennant in 1944.

The Monarchs' Winning Ways

Meantime, across the state from the Browns, the Kansas City Monarchs were becoming the toast of the Negro National League. Led by Wilber "Bullet Joe" Rogan, the Monarchs went 50–31 in 1921 to finish a close second behind the Chicago American Giants. Rogan, an outstanding pitcher with a tremendous fastball, a fine curve, and good control, starred for the Monarchs for almost twenty years. The short right-hander was a workhorse, averaging thirty games per year for a decade without ever being relieved. Despite Rogan's best efforts, however, the Monarchs dipped to third place in 1922, but in 1923 the team cruised to the league championship with a 57–33 record.

In 1924 the Monarchs again took the Negro National League, finishing at 55–22, but this time there was a new wrinkle: a postseason championship series. In 1922 a group of eastern businessmen had formed the Eastern Colored League. After intense rivalry for a year, in 1924 the leaders of the two leagues decided to organize the first championship series between the winners of the two league pennants. Billed as the first Colored World Series, the Monarchs faced off against the Philadelphia Hilldales in a rugged championship series. The Monarchs came out on top in the series, winning five of nine games.

In 1925 the Monarchs again won the Negro National League. That year, the league decided to divide the season into two halves. The Monarchs won outright in the first half of the season and finished second in the second half, for an overall record of 62–23. To claim the league championship they had to defeat the season's second-half winner, the St. Louis Stars. The winner would face the Hilldales again in the Colored World Series. The Stars, led by the legendary outfielder James Thomas "Cool Papa" Bell—rumored to be the fastest man alive—proved to be tough competitors, but eventually fell to the Monarchs in a grueling seven-game series. The Monarchs then lost to the Hilldales five games to one.

In 1926 the Monarchs again had the best record in the Negro National League, finishing at 57–21. They played the Chicago American Giants, winner of one-half of the season, for the privilege of returning to the Colored World Series. But their pennant-winning streak ended at the hands of Chicago, as Giants pitcher Willie Foster beat Rogan twice to clinch the series. The Monarchs remained a powerhouse in the Negro National League for the rest of the decade, but both their fortunes and those of the league took a decided turn for the worse with the coming of the Great Depression in 1929. Indeed, the league collapsed in 1930.

The Monarchs and some of the other league teams returned to barnstorming for survival. Five years before the major leagues turned on any lights, in 1929, the Kansas City Monarchs became the first team to regularly play night baseball. Monarchs owner J. L. Wilkinson bought a portable-lighting system so the team could play at night on the road. This proved both a safety net and a godsend for the team. The ability to rent a playing field for an evening game ensured both a place to hold the game and an audience. The system consisted of a set of telescoping poles, which elevated lights fifty feet above the field. Each pole supported six floodlights measuring four feet across. Affixed by means of a pivot on a truck bed and raised with a derrick, the lights ringed the outfield and the grandstand. A 250-horsepower motor powered the system, and the whole thing could be set up in two hours and taken down in less than one.

The Monarchs struggled through the depression, and only became a truly excellent box office attraction again as the decade of the 1930s came to a close. In 1937 the Monarchs joined the newly created Negro American League and won the championship over the Chicago entry. They won again in 1939 by besting the St. Louis franchise three games to two in a playoff, and then went on to other league pennants in 1940, 1941, and 1942. In that first year of World War II the Monarchs played the Homestead Grays in the first Colored World Series since 1927. They steamrolled the Grays, with their great catcher Josh Gibson, four games to none. This was possible largely because of the addition of pitcher Leroy "Satchel" Paige and first baseman John "Buck" O'Neil. Paige was the greatest star ever to arise in the Negro Leagues, eventually making his way to the Cleveland Indians in 1948 and helping them to win the World Series that year. The lanky right-hander with the marvelous fastball (and a host of other colorfully named pitches), nimble wit, and effervescent personality made himself into a household name recognized by people who knew little about baseball, and even less about the Negro Leagues. His name became synonymous with the barnstorming exhibitions played between traveling black teams and their white counterparts. With four championships in five years, the Monarchs were truly the monarchs—pun intended—of African American baseball. Although their run of championships ended in 1943, the Monarchs continued to dominate the Negro American League until its collapse in 1960, thirteen years after the desegregation of the major leagues and long after the best of its talent had been raided to stock the formerly all-white teams.

Satchel Paige was the greatest pitcher of the Negro Leagues. His baseball career spanned twenty-seven years with the Kansas City Monarchs and other teams. His legendary actions spanned a much longer time frame. Courtesy of Classicphotos.com, Ely, Minnesota.

The Rise of a Cardinal Dynasty

If from the mid-1920s to the mid-1950s you were to ask almost any man or woman on the street in the Midwest, Great Plains, South, or Far West to name their favorite baseball team, they would invariably talk about the St. Louis Cardinals. During this period St. Louis was the farthest west and south of any major-league city, and automatically attracted the attention of baseball fans in those regions. But it was more than that. The Cardinals rose to prominence, captured the allegiances of those in the great heartland of America, and some would say never released it. The quality of the team's play and the scrappiness of the players sealed the love affair.

The attraction was almost magical. Journalist Warner Fusselle remembered nostalgically how as a boy growing up in Lynchburg, Virginia, home to a low-level Cardinals farm team, he became a fan. He went to see those young minor leaguers every chance he got and followed their progress to the big leagues, but he also searched the airwaves on a 1946 RCA tabletop radio each night for the powerful KMOX radio station that broadcast the Cardinals' games. Listening to Harry Caray, the voice of the Cardinals for more than twenty years beginning in the 1940s, Fusselle became obsessed with the Cards—the universal pet name for the team—and basked in their reflected glory.

Until the mid-1920s *the* team to follow in the region had not been the Cardinals but the Browns. This only changed when Branch Rickey moved to the Cardinals and his "farm system" strategy began to produce winning teams. Supported enthusiastically by the Cardinals' owner, St. Louis automobile dealer Sam Breadon, Rickey immediately implemented his farm system by purchasing controlling interests in five minor-league teams, stocking them with players who would be instructed in the finer points of the game. By 1936 the Cardinals owned controlling interests in twenty-eight minor-league franchises scattered throughout the nation, a dozen more than any other major-league team. At its peak, Rickey's farm system included thirty-three teams. In contrast, each major-league franchise today operates only five or six minor-league teams.

The farm clubs proved enormously productive for the Cardinals. Indicative of its method of operation were two young men from southern Illinois who tried out for the Cardinals in 1917 at one of the open tryouts sponsored at regular intervals throughout the year for its nascent farm system. One of these men was my paternal grandfather, Jeff Hilliard Launius; the other was a friend, Ray Blades. The Cardinals offered both of them minor-league contracts tiny in terms of money, but enormous in the opportunity to prove their mettle and perhaps to eventually make the big-league team. Both returned home to their families to discuss the opportunity. Jeff Launius's mother questioned whether this was even legitimate work and urged him to pursue a more common work path. She also begged him not to sign because it would necessitate playing baseball on Sundays, which ran against her strict religious ideals. Because of this he chose not to pursue a career in baseball and settled down to become a farmer, living a long and generally rewarding life.

But Jeff Launius always regretted not signing that contract. When I was a small boy he told me the story more than once of how he agonized over his decision and eventually acceded to his mother's wishes. His good friend signed, went into the Cardinals farm system, and in 1922 made the major leagues. Ray Blades played with the Cardinals for ten seasons, becoming an integral part of the championship teams of 1926, 1928, 1930, and 1931, and later manager of the team in 1939–1940. Perhaps it was braggadocio, but Jeff Launius always said that he was as good a player as Blades and could have enjoyed equal or even greater success on the field. Despite his regret, Jeff Launius was a lifelong Cardinals fan, and so seemed everyone else in the sleepy town of McLeansboro, Illinois, about one hundred miles from St. Louis, where he lived out his life. Indeed, one would have to look long and hard anywhere in the region to find someone who did not claim allegiance to the Cardinals. They were that enticing.

The different lives of Jeff Launius and Ray Blades illustrate the serendipity of careers in baseball, but also the great rigor of the Cardinal player development system as Branch Rickey constructed it. Without question, the high quality of players emerging from that farm system established the Cardinals as *the* team to beat in the National League. The system produced Hall of Famers such as first baseman Jim Bottomley (a Cardinal from 1922–1932 with a .310 career batting average and 219 career home runs), pitcher Dizzy Dean (1930, 1932–1937, 150 career wins, 83 career losses), left fielder Chick Hafey (1924–1931, .317 career batting average, 164 career home runs), pitcher Jesse Haines (1920–1937, 210 career wins, 158 career losses), second baseman Rogers Hornsby, (1915–1926, 1933, .358 career batting average, 301 career home runs), left fielder Joe Medwick (1932–1940, 1947–1948, .324 career batting average, 204 career home runs), first baseman Johnny Mize (1936–1941, .312 career batting average, 359 career home runs), and right fielder Enos Slaughter (1938–1942, 1946–1953, .300 career batting average, 169 career home runs).

The greatest Cardinal of them all, of course, was Stan "The Man" Musial, a sore-armed left-handed pitcher whose retreading into an outfielder proved perhaps the most fortunate transformation of any player since Babe Ruth moved from the pitcher's mound to left field for good in 1919. In a stunning twenty-two-year career, The Man (no other identification is necessary) racked up a .331 career batting average and won the batting title seven times, hit 475 career home runs, hit safely 3,630 times, was named Most Valuable Player in the National League three times, perennially played on the National League All-Star teams, and upon retirement held seventeen major-league, twenty-nine National League, and nine All-Star Game records. His career represented the pinnacle of the great Cardinals' farm system. Musial's career was also one of great dignity and poetry both on and off the field, and he remains an icon in St. Louis long after his retirement in 1963.

The Cardinals began their rise to glory in the mid-1920s. Early in the 1925 season, with the Cards in last place and Branch Rickey as both general and field manager, Breadon reassigned Rickey full-time to the front office and replaced him on the field with second baseman Rogers Hornsby. Hornsby, whose career batting average of .358 remains second only to Ty Cobb's, is universally believed to be the greatest right-handed hitter of all time. By 1925 he had already become legendary in St. Louis; the year before he had hit .424—the highest single-season batting average of the twentieth century—and indeed from 1921–1925, his cumulative batting average was .402, a truly amazing accomplishment.

Hall of Famer Rogers Hornsby was the second baseman and manager of the St. Louis Cardinals in the mid-1920s. He led the Cardinals to their first pennant and World Series title in 1926, over the New York Yankees. Courtesy of Classicphotos.com, Ely, Minnesota.

The managerial switch to Hornsby worked. The Cardinals finished 1925 in fourth place, then captured their first pennant in 1926 by edging Cincinnati in the final week of the season. The season was made perfect by a World Series victory over Babe Ruth and the New York Yankees. The series opened in New York, with the Yankees taking a narrow 2–1 victory, but the Cardinals stormed back to take the next two games. The Yankees then won Games Four and Five, but in the sixth game veteran pitcher Grover Cleveland "Pete" Alexander, nearing the end of an illustrious but drink-befouled career, scattered eight hits while the Cards teed off on the Yankees' hurlers for a 10–2 romp.

This set up a dramatic seventh game to decide the series. Alexander, possibly sleeping off a hangover in the bullpen, barely noticed that the Cardinals and starting pitcher Jesse Haines enjoyed a 3–2 lead over the Yankees and Waite Hoyt in the seventh inning. Haines weakened in the last of the seventh, however, and gave up three walks to put Earle Combs, Bob Meusel, and Lou Gehrig on base with two out and Tony Lazzeri at the plate. At that point Hornsby decided to put in Alexander. On a 1–1 count Lazzeri hit a line drive into the left-field seats and the crowd let out a roar, thinking that the Yanks were going to win another one. But the ball landed just a few feet to the foul side of the pole. When Alexander served up another, Lazzeri swung for the fences again but missed for strike three. Alexander then mowed down the Yanks in order until Babe Ruth drew a walk with two out in the ninth inning. Amazingly, he tried to steal second base and was thrown out to end the game. The Cards had their first World Championship. Each Cardinal player collected $5,584.51 for the victory, while the Yankees received $3,417.75 each. St. Louisians were as proud as they could possibly be, and the Cardinals' dominance of the city's baseball fans had begun.

Two months after the Cards' great triumph, on December 20, 1926, Rickey traded Hornsby to the New York Giants for Frankie Frisch and Jimmy Ring after repeated disputes between Hornsby and owner Sam Breadon. The Cardinals finished in second place in 1927, but rebounded in 1928 to take the pennant again. This time, however, the outcome was far different, as the Yankees swept them in four straight World Series games. They took the pennant again in 1930, shooting from a losing record in mid-June to thirty games above .500 by season's end and overtaking three other teams to clinch the flag just three games before the season's finish. The Cardinals lost in the World Series to an exceptional Philadelphia Athletics team, four games to two. Still, the Cardinals had won three pennants in five years.

But they were far from done. In 1931 the Cardinals put on the field what many consider their best team ever. They won 101 games, leading the National League the entire season and finishing thirteen games in front of their nearest challengers. Frankie Frisch had become the club's heart and soul, and captured the league's Most Valuable Player award. Two other Cardinals, Chick Hafey and Sunny Jim Bottomley, battled all season for the batting title. When the dust settled, they were within a point of each other. Hafey came out on top with a .3489 average. Remarkably, Bottomley came in third at .3481, with the Giants' Bill Terry between them. The pitching was anchored by Wild Bill Hallahan, whose nickname belied his excellent control. At 19–9, he tied for the league's victory

Dizzy Dean and his brother, Paul "Daffy" Dean, were the heart and soul of the Cardinals' pitching staff in 1934. Here they pose for photos before the World Series, in which each won two games to lead St. Louis to the world championship. Courtesy of the Missouri Historical Society, St. Louis.

lead. Paul Derringer and Burleigh Grimes won 18 and 17 games respectively. Four of the league's top five base stealers, including league leader Frisch and rookie outfielder Pepper Martin, were Cardinals.

The 1931 World Series brought a rematch with the Philadelphia Athletics. The Athletics, World Champions in 1929 and 1930, had won 107 regular-season games and seemed destined to become the first team ever to take three straight

World Series titles. But the Cardinals prevailed. Sparked by Martin, the Cardinals hung tough and outdueled Philadelphia in seven games to capture their second World Championship.

When the Cards dropped to sixth place in 1932 and showed little sign of improvement the following year, Rickey began to play doctor with the franchise. He traded players and changed managers to find a winning combination. He sent Bottomley to the Cubs and Hafey to the Reds. He acquired Leo "the Lip" Durocher, famous for his cutting tongue, from the Reds to play shortstop. And he brought up from the farm system Jerome (sometimes called Jay) "Dizzy" Dean, a young, handsome, tall-tale teller with even more self-confidence than his considerable skills justified, to anchor the pitching staff. "Ol' Diz's" younger brother, Paul, christened "Daffy" by the sportswriters, soon found his way up from the farm as well. Rickey also replaced manager Gabby Street with Frankie Frisch. These changes brought results.

During the 1934 spring training camp, Dizzy Dean told a journalist that "me 'n' Paul will win 45 to 50 games." When asked how many of the fifty he would win, Dizzy replied that he would win those that Paul didn't. The Cards did win, and the brothers Dean did as well, Dizzy going 30–7 and Paul 19–11. They pitched the team to a pennant, supported by a stellar cast of roughnecks. It was tight race for most of the year, and the Cards had to win thirteen of their final fifteen games to pass the front-running New York Giants in the final week of the season. Of the team's final nine wins, Dizzy and Paul accounted for seven.

Writers labeled the 1934 Cardinals the "Gashouse Gang" for their rowdy and daring play. In addition to team veterans Frisch and Martin (who had been shifted from the outfield to third base), the gang included Durocher at shortstop, left fielder Joe "Ducky" Medwick, and the team's leading hitter and slugger, first baseman Rip Collins, who in a career-best season led the league in slugging average and tied for first in home runs. In a seven-game World Series, the Cardinals prevailed, and the Dean boys won them all, each getting a pair of victories in the Cards' triumph over the Detroit Tigers.

Through the rest of the 1930s the Cardinals were competitive, but not victors. Changes had to come again. In the closing days of the 1941 season, the farm system's greatest product arrived at the big club: Stan Musial. The next year—Musial's first full season—the Cardinals enjoyed their winningest season ever, with 106 victories. They needed them all, too, for the Brooklyn Dodgers won 104 games. Brooklyn, which had won the pennant a year earlier, had a ten-game lead in early August, but St. Louis caught fire the last two months, winning forty-three of their final fifty-one games—and twelve of their final thirteen—to

Press cameramen and movie operators perched on the roof of the upper deck at Sportsman's Park to photograph plays during the 1934 World Series between St. Louis and Detroit. The long-focus camera operator in the foreground had to maintain his strained crouched position all through the game. Courtesy of the Missouri Historical Society, St. Louis.

catch and surpass the Dodgers. When the dust settled, the Cardinals were two games ahead.

St. Louis pitchers Mort Cooper and Johnny Beazley finished one-two in the National League in wins and earned run average. Cooper, the league's Most Valuable Player, was 22–7 with a league-best 1.77 ERA. Beazley finished 21–6 and had a 2.14 ERA. Musial was a twenty-one-year-old rookie, but he made an immediate impact with a .315 batting average. He joined Terry Moore and Enos Slaughter in the outfield. Slaughter batted .318, led the league in hits, and ranked among the league's leaders in runs batted in and runs scored. The club maintained its momentum through the World Series, taking the Yankees in five games. The last series of the pre–World War II era found Beazley winning twice and Whitey Kurowski driving in five runs.

Stan "The Man" Musial in his classic batting stance. Courtesy of
Classicphotos.com, Ely, Minnesota.

In the ensuing days, months, and years, players would begin entering the
armed forces in World War II. The war's impact on major-league rosters in 1942
had been minimal. Yet during the off-season, a great number of ballplayers were
called to service. Slaughter, Moore, and Beazley missed the next three years, and
many others such as Musial missed at least one season.

The Cardinals won three more pennants and two World Series championships
in the 1940s. In 1943 they lost a rematch of the previous year's World Series, falling to the Yankees. After the series, most of the Yankees and Cardinals
game caps were shipped to the South Pacific, where Major "Pappy" Boyington

Enos Slaughter nailed down one of the three outfield spots in the Cardinals outfield of the 1940s. Slaughter, Musial, and Terry Moore formed one of the best outfields ever to play the game. Courtesy of the Missouri State Archives.

promised one to any pilot in his group who shot down a Japanese Zero. Ten percent of the World Series proceeds given to the players were paid in war bonds. In 1946, the Cards beat the Boston Red Sox, playing in their first World Series since 1918, four games to three.

The Great Streetcar Series of 1944

But it was the 1944 World Series that captured the hearts of most Missourians. In that year both the Cardinals and the Browns took their respective league pennants and met in the World Series. The Cardinal win was expected by almost everyone, and the team won 105 games and ran away with the pennant. No question, the Cards were the class of the National League. But the Browns surprised everyone by taking the American League pennant despite winning a mere 85 games. *Even the Browns* was the original title of William B. Mead's superb book on wartime baseball (*Baseball Goes to War*), a suggestion that the level of competition in the major leagues during wartime was suspect. Thus "even the Browns" were good enough to win a pennant. The team had been so woeful since the late 1920s that many of the team's fans considered it a badge of honor—even a statement of machismo—to root for the hapless team. They took pride in the generally apt St. Louis descriptor, "First in shoes, first in booze, and last in the American League." In reality, the Browns rebuilt themselves into a decent team during this period, posting three winning seasons in the war years 1942–1945. They finished a distant third in 1942 before finally winning their only St. Louis pennant by edging the Detroit Tigers on the final day of the season after trailing them through most of September.

But the Browns survived that tough pennant race only to win the honor of playing sacrificial lamb for a truly outstanding Cardinals team. The Cards were so overwhelmingly favored in the World Series that it is doubtful if any serious people wagered against them. Cardinals shortstop Marty Marion later reflected, "If the Browns had beat us, that would have really been a disgrace."

The 1944 World Series represented the only postseason contest involving Missouri teams from the same city. Common in New York, especially between the Yankees and the Giants, a "streetcar" series was virtually unheard of elsewhere in the country. Only in 1906, when Chicago's Cubs and White Sox met in the World Series, had a streetcar series taken place outside of New York. As such, this unusual occurrence captured the attention of the public. For Missourians, only the 1985 World Series between the Cardinals and the cross-state Kansas City Royals would equal the 1944 series for interest and drama.

The championship series was filled with ironies. Both the Browns and the Cards shared Sportsman's Park in St. Louis, which was owned by the Browns; the far more successful Cardinals were their tenants. Moreover, with the wartime shortage of housing the two teams' managers, the Browns' Luke Sewell and the Cardinals' Billy Southworth, shared an apartment in the city during the year. This was convenient because when the Cards were in town, the Browns were on the road, and vice versa. Finally, the Cardinals, long considered the best of the

St. Louis Browns owner Donald Barnes is surrounded by his players after the team clinched its only American League pennant in 1944. The shirtless wonder without the washboard stomach in the center is Sig Jakucki, winning pitcher in the deciding game of the pennant race. It is unfortunate that the Browns faced one of the greatest teams in baseball history, the 1940s-era Cardinals, in the World Series and lost in six games. Courtesy of the Missouri Historical Society, St. Louis.

National League teams, had a roster filled with stars whose fingers were weighed down with championship rings, while the Browns had long been the doormats of the American League. It was a series not to be missed.

And the American Leaguers put on a good show. The Browns' George Mc-Quinn led all hitters in the series with a .438 average and two homers, and the pitching staff posted a 1.46 ERA. Conversely, the Cardinals' best hitter in the series was second baseman Emil Verban, who batted .412. He had been considered such a non-threat at the plate that the Browns' pitchers neglected even to discuss how to pitch to him prior to the series. Cards catcher Walker Cooper also batted .318, devastating the Browns at seemingly every turn. Collectively, the Browns batted a mere .183, struck out 43 times, and committed 10 errors. The Cards, on the other hand, tied the mark for fewest errors in a six-game series (one).

Neither team stole a base, a rarity especially for the Cards, and also a record for a six-game series.

In Game One the Browns prevailed 2–1, perhaps because the Cardinals under-estimated their opponent. In Game Two it took the Cardinals eleven innings to win 3–2 and tie the series. The Browns then pounded the Cardinals 6–2 in Game Three as pitcher Jack Kramer silenced the National Leaguers by striking out ten and not allowing an earned run. The Browns' offense offered ample support by scoring three times with two out in the fourth inning on five consecutive singles, then adding two more runs in the seventh on doubles from Don Gutteridge and McQuinn. But over the final three games of the series, the Browns scored only two more runs. The Cards won Game Four 5–1 to tie the series, and then went on to win the final two games as well, 2–0 and 3–1. As the streetcar series ended, it took with it the last opportunity for the Browns to produce a winner in St. Louis. After a good season in 1945, they slid back into their normal place at the bottom of the league until their departure to Baltimore in 1953.

Without question the major-league teams of Missouri became contenders and champions during the 1920s and remained so into the 1940s. In many respects the era represented the high point of success for the Cardinals, Browns, and Monarchs. But a long dry spell was coming. After their 1946 World Series win over the Boston Red Sox, the Cardinals would not appear in postseason play again until 1964. The Browns would never again play in the World Series and would soon leave the state for good. And with the integration of major-league baseball in 1947, the Monarchs would suffer a slow decline as the team's best players moved to the American and National Leagues.

A Long Dry Spell in the Midwest

Between 1947 and 1964 no Missouri major-league team won a championship, or even a pennant, and the nature of baseball in the state fundamentally changed. First, in 1953 the Browns left St. Louis for Baltimore, where they renamed themselves the Orioles and eventually became one of the most successful teams in baseball history. Second, the Monarchs ceased to exist. With the integration of professional baseball in 1947, the best players in the Negro Leagues began to leave their teams. While virtually everyone views integration as a positive step, it spelled the doom of the Negro Leagues. The Monarchs were a casualty of that process. Finally, in 1955 the Philadelphia Athletics, a perennial doormat in the American League since the 1930s, moved to Kansas City, where they continued their losing tradition until moving farther west, to Oakland, California.

The Demise of the Browns

One can reach several reasonable conclusions about the rivalry between the two major-league baseball teams in St. Louis. First, the Browns and the Cardinals were attempting to share a pie that grew ever smaller, as throughout the first half of the twentieth century their city declined in population relative to other major-league cities. That meant that it was only a matter of time before one team or the other would have to depart from St. Louis.

Second, because of the stagnant population base, the Browns and Cardinals had to compete mightily for the limited dollars available for major-league base-ball in St. Louis. Competition took place on a broad front. Since baseball is essentially a part of the entertainment industry, delivering a good time to the

The window of a downtown St. Louis department store in the late 1940s showed the pride felt by the city for its two baseball teams. Courtesy of the State Historical Society of Missouri, Columbia.

spectators is critical to the success of a franchise. This can most effectively be accomplished by putting good teams on the field. Without question the Cardinals ruled in this arena, at least after 1926, and they accordingly captured the loyalties of most of the city's baseball fans. In 1926, for instance, the Cardinals won the pennant and had an attendance of 506,000 for the season. The Browns' attendance was a woeful 81,000. To demonstrate this discrepancy further, in 1935 the Browns averaged only 1,051 in paid attendance per game. Until the Cardinals, buttressed by the brilliance of Branch Rickey's farm system, began to dominate the National League, the Browns had competed very well for the baseball dollar in St. Louis.

Even without fielding a great team, attendance at games could be enhanced by offering other types of attractions. Bill Veeck, owner of the Browns in their final seasons, was a master of this, as Chris Von der Ahe had been in the 1880s. In 1952 Veeck doubled attendance at Browns games over the previous year by offering "bread and circuses" in the stands to offset the woeful team on the field. But it was a case of too little too late.

The Cardinals also froze the Browns out of the extended family of supporters in the Midwest and the South. When radio began to make an impact on the sport in the mid-1920s, the Cardinals quickly became adept at using the new medium to expand the team's fan base. After routinely broadcasting re-creations of its games in the late 1920s and early 1930s, in 1934 the Cardinals decided not to broadcast regular games. Despite an exciting pennant-winning team, season attendance fell 283,000 below that of the previous pennant-winner in 1931. Accordingly, the organization restored its regular-season radio broadcasts.

By the time of the Cardinals dynasty of the 1940s, the team boasted a regional network of 120 stations in nine states, anchored by powerful KMOX in St. Louis. From the Great Plains to the Deep South, the St. Louis Cardinals became the team most people of the heartland supported, and thousands of fans made bus trips to St. Louis to see Cardinals games. The voice of the Cardinals from 1945 until 1969 was the irascible St. Louis–born Harry Caray. Millions tuned in to hear his stirring accounts of the play of the boys in red.

Two questions that must be asked about the Browns and the Cardinals are: "Is there any evidence that certain groups followed one or the other of the teams?" and "What was the ethnic, class, or other demographic loyalty for the St. Louis teams at various periods of time?" From the beginning, both teams were largely Irish-American, and the large German/American constituency in the city embraced them. That close relationship remained throughout the Browns/ Cardinals era. Neither team gained a widespread following from the African American community, which reserved its loyalties for the Negro Leagues teams.

But there was more than ethnic attachment behind the Cardinals' attraction. The Cardinals became the embodiment of the American heartland in a way the Browns never did. The Cards were hayseeds, just like most of the people who supported them. They represented rural America—simplicity, rusticity, small towns, Protestant beliefs, and hard-working commoners—and the fact that they often won against the big-city Giants and Yankees added to their appeal. The Cardinals' best players, from Dizzy Dean to Stan Musial, personified these perceived virtues as well.

There is a Hollywood formula for successful war movies, and from *The Sands of Iwo Jima* to *Saving Private Ryan* it has been played out in most of them. The cast of soldiers represents a cross-section of America: streetwise punks from Brooklyn or Newark, farm boys from the Midwest, country boys from the South, and city slickers from New York. The audiences identify with these characters depending on background and familiarity. Similar allegiances are at play in major-league baseball. While the Brooklyn Dodgers might have represented working-class urbanites and the Yankees reflected the glitter of New York's upper class, the Cardinals represented the midwestern farming culture and the southern backcountry. To the extent that they were successful, and they were very successful during the second quarter of the century, the Cardinals served to heighten these regions' collective spirit.

Finally, the Cardinals were able to force the Browns out of St. Louis because of two horrendous decisions made by the Browns' ownership. First, in 1917 Browns' owner Philip C. Ball pushed Branch Rickey out of his organization. Rickey promptly went across town to the Cardinals, where his farm system resulted in Cardinals domination for the next generation. Had Ball left Rickey alone, the Browns might have become the big winner.

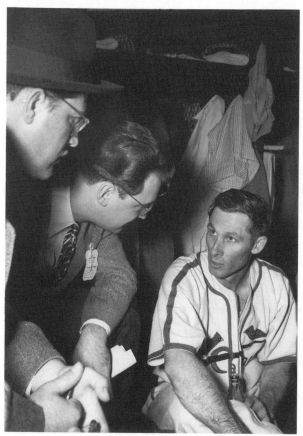

The Cardinals were quick to develop a powerful regional radio network of 120 stations in nine states, anchored by powerful KMOX in St. Louis. The voice of the Cardinals from the 1940s through the 1960s was Harry Caray. Here a young, bespectacled Caray interviews Cardinals pitcher Harry Brecheen in 1948. Courtesy of the Missouri State Archives.

Second, when the Cardinals' wooden ballpark burned down in 1920, Rickey persuaded Ball to grant the National League team a long-term lease for state-of-the-art, concrete-and-steel Sportsman's Park. Henceforth, the Cardinals shared the park with the Browns for longer than any other two teams, until 1953. Had Ball said no, the Cardinals, who had no ready capital with which to build their own ballpark, would have been forced to seek a home elsewhere, perhaps somewhere other than in St. Louis. In an irony too great to ignore, the Browns' owner sowed the seeds of his team's own demise in 1920, although it took more than thirty years for the team to reach its nadir. In the end, St. Louis was not big enough for both teams.

In 1944 the St. Louis Browns won the American League pennant with a mediocre record of 89–65, a winning percentage of .578. Had they played in the National League that year, the Browns' season record would only have been good enough to tie with the Cincinnati Reds for third place, a distant sixteen games behind the Cardinals. Matched up against their powerful cross-town rivals in the World Series, it was not surprising that the Browns lost. When the series was over, Cardinals owner Sam Breadon expressed relief, saying, "If we'd have lost this Series to the Browns, I'd have had to leave town. It would have been a disgrace to lose to the Browns."

Perhaps, but the Browns' leadership anticipated that 1945 would be another good year for the team, and many believed in its chances to repeat as American League champions. The Browns were weak on offense, batting just .252 as a team in 1944, but they were built on strong pitching, excellent defense, and unusual camaraderie, all of which figured to carry over to the 1945 season. Browns manager Luke Sewell characterized his team as "a fairly representative club for the war years . . . combative and highly competitive."

Despite high hopes, however, the Browns started the 1945 season slowly, quickly slipping to seventh place, and they looked to be en route to another year in the American League's second division. They recovered, however, and finished in third place, with a respectable 81–70 record, just six games behind the league-champion Detroit Tigers. They would never finish so high in the standings again.

The 1945 Browns season was far more memorable for the debut of the player sportswriters dubbed the "one-armed wonder," Pete Gray. Born Peter J. Wyshner in the grimy coal-mining town of Nanticoke, Pennsylvania, Gray at age six lost his right arm in a farming accident. He showed remarkable perseverance, however, and pursued sports with a zeal born of adversity. He overcame his handicap to play semi-pro and later professional ball. In 1943 and 1944 he played for the

Class A Southern Association's Memphis Chicks. After hitting a solid .299 in 1943, he blossomed into a star the following year. In 1944 he hit .333, drove in 60 runs, stole 63 bases, led the league in fielding percentage, and was voted the Southern Association's most valuable player. While his handicap certainly raised questions about his ability to play in the major leagues, his 1944 performance earned him a serious look. The Browns acquired his contract for twenty thousand dollars. Manager Sewell viewed Gray as a spark plug whose bat and speed would stimulate the Browns' pitiful offense. His fielding could only help in the outfield. The one-armed outfielder was also expected to be a gate attraction, especially for thousands of men returning from World War II with handicaps just as significant as Gray's.

For his part, Gray understood that he was something of a token acquisition for the team, and spoke diplomatically about his goals during spring training:

> I surely am going to give it everything I have. I want to make good, not only for myself, but for the Browns. I hope I can make a lot of money for them, for they are willing to give me my big chance. I know I've got to make good to be an attraction, but I know thousands of people are rooting for me. I get letters and good wishes from fans all over the country. A lot of them come from servicemen. They'll be watching to see what I do in the box scores, and if I make the team, there will be a lot of them out to see me play.

Sewell cut Gray no slack during spring training, but when the regular season began, Gray was in the lineup as the lead-off hitter, and that is where he stayed for most of the year. "He surely gets a good piece of the ball, is unusually fast, and it is fascinating to see what he can do with that one arm," Sewell said. The manager promised to give Gray "every opportunity to make the grade," and he kept his word.

Gray had some spectacular moments. He beat the Tigers virtually by himself during their first lash-up of the season. A reporter with the *Detroit News* opined in June 1945 that no one could any longer be suspicious of the Browns' owner for "hiring the outfielder for box office purposes. That he helps the gate receipts is inevitable, but that he helped the Browns win games now is evident to all who have watched him play." Gray did help at the gate. By July 1945 the Browns had won over many die-hard Cardinals fans through the sympathy and excitement generated by Gray's presence in a Browns uniform. Fans came to games at Sportsman's Park in droves; 150,000 more paid attendees saw the Browns play through the end of May than had attended games through the end of May 1944.

Unfortunately for Gray and the Browns, the "one-armed wonder" could not sustain his early season success. Once opposing pitchers found his weakness,

The St. Louis Browns management thought that one-armed outfielder Pete Gray would stimulate the team's pitiful offense. Gray, the Southern Association's Most Valuable Player in 1944, found the majors in 1945 a much tougher place. As the Browns' lead-off hitter, he managed only a .218 batting mark. Courtesy of the Missouri Historical Society, St. Louis.

they were merciless. Since Gray had only one arm, he had to start the bat earlier than most other hitters, and he had less control over it once he began his swing. He had become a star in the Southern Association by murdering fastballs, and he could hit big-league ones as well, but he had trouble with curves and change-ups because of his difficulty in altering the bat during his swing. Appearing in seventy-seven games for the Browns, Gray batted just .218 with 51 hits in 234 plate appearances. Sewell finally benched him when his hitting tapered off.

In an irony of the first magnitude, the noble experiment of giving a one-armed ballplayer a major-league opportunity may have cost the Browns the pennant. While his teammates admired Gray's courage and resolution, several blamed their third-place finish on him. According to third baseman Mark Christman:

> Pete did a great job with what he had. But he cost us the pennant in 1945. We finished third, only six games out. There were an awful lot of ground balls hit to center field. When the kids who hit those balls were pretty good runners, they could keep on going and wind up at second base [because Gray could not throw the ball in as fast as a two-armed player]. I know that lost us eight or ten ball games because it took away the double play or somebody would single and the runner on second would score, where if he had been on first it would take two hits to get him to score.

Browns first baseman George McQuinn echoed that view:

> Even though Pete Gray was a miracle man in a lot of ways, he still could not do as good a job as a guy with two arms, let's face it. He couldn't field ground balls or flies or shift his glove quickly enough to get the ball back to the infield as fast as the average man. There's no question that he cost us quite a few ball games.

When the Browns' 1945 season ended, so did the major-league career of Pete Gray. Thereafter he played with several minor-league clubs all over the country before retiring to his hometown of Nanticoke in 1949.

In the seasons after 1945, the Browns slid in the standings, finally losing more than a hundred games in 1949. The Browns were pathetic and seemed to be on the road either to indescribable ruin or to another city. In one series with the Red Sox in 1950, known as the "Boston Massacre," the Browns lost back-to-back games by scores of 20–4 and 29–4, the worst slaughter in American League history. How could the team get any worse? It did in 1951, losing 102 games and finishing 46 games behind the pennant-winning Yankees. The only bright spot was the pitching of Ned Garver, who went 20–12 for a team that won only 52 games. The next spring when Garver wanted a big salary hike because of his banner year, the owner returned the contract to him with a note that read, "We could have finished last without you!" Garver signed for twenty-five thousand dollars.

The 1951 season was notable in Browns history for the coming of a new owner, the indomitable Bill Veeck. The much-traveled Veeck, perhaps the only populist

In a moment orchestrated to conjure recollections of Branch Rickey's signing of Jackie Robinson for the Brooklyn Dodgers, Browns' owner Bill Veeck looks on as legendary Satchel Paige signs a contract to play for St. Louis in 1951. Courtesy of the Missouri Historical Society, St. Louis.

owner in major-league baseball history, assumed a controlling interest in the team on July 5, 1951, when it was 23 1/2 games out of first place. He immediately set out to remake the Browns into a crowd pleaser, if not a pennant winner. Veeck, the son of a Chicago Cubs general manager, had grown up in baseball and is fabled to have planted the ivy along the outfield wall at Wrigley Field. He held a succession of jobs with the Cubs, then in the early 1940s bought a controlling interest in the minor-league Milwaukee Brewers. He hosted stunts and oversaw practical jokes during the games; he pioneered the now ubiquitous giveaway days at ballparks for everything from bats to beer steins. Once he entertained his Milwaukee fans with a gadget to raise the outfield fences of his stadium when the visiting team batted and lower them when his team was at the plate. That stunt lasted one game; the next day the league banned its use. All of this was concocted solely to entertain his paying customers.

Veeck was above all else a master showman, and his ability to promote and excite fans always served him well. His philosophy was simple: more people will pay to see a bad team that has stunts and giveaways than will pay to see just a bad team. So he worked hard to make every game an entertaining, even zany, experience. Fans who leave the game with smiles on their faces will come back, he reasoned. But he was also a genius at building winners, and his Milwaukee team took three minor-league pennants in five years.

After selling the Brewers in 1945, Veeck bought a controlling interest in the Cleveland Indians and transformed them into a powerhouse, all the while entertaining his customers with bread and circuses. The Indians won the World Series in 1948 and became perennial contenders thereafter. In 1954, after Veeck sold the team but while his presence was still very apparent, the Indians won another pennant—with an incredible record of 111–43—but lost in the World Series.

Veeck was also an early and persistent advocate of baseball's integration. He signed Larry Doby from the Kansas City Monarchs, and Doby became the American League's first black star when he arrived in Cleveland near the end of the 1947 season. The next year Veeck signed another Monarch, the legendary Satchel Paige, who as a forty-two-year-old rookie went 6–1 for the Indians during their pennant-winning season.

When Veeck arrived in St. Louis he vowed to rebuild the Browns, entertain the fans, and drive the Cardinals from the city, not necessarily in that order. He immediately set out to annoy the Cardinals owners, and he proved a master at it. He repainted Sportsman's Park, which the Browns still owned and rented to the Cardinals, in his team's colors and decorated it with Brownie memorabilia. At one point he prohibited the Cardinals from flying their league championship and World Series pennants in the stadium.

Veeck also hired several former Cardinals legends to work for the Browns, to irritate the Cardinals management and to win fans from the city rivals. The most important of these was Rogers Hornsby, who managed the Browns during the first part of 1952. Marty Marion, another Cardinals great, replaced Hornsby in midseason. Dizzy Dean, the Hall of Fame Cardinals pitcher, also worked for the Browns as a radio sportscaster. These moves all irked the Cardinals, just as intended.

Veeck quickly sought out African American players, in striking contrast to the Cardinals, who were among the last teams in major-league baseball to integrate. The Browns had integrated even before Veeck, signing two players from the Kansas City Monarchs in 1947. Hard-hitting outfielder Willard J. Brown and infielder Hank Thompson each had "a cup of coffee" with the Browns in 1947, but neither player was able to stick. Brown went an unimpressive 10 for 67 at the plate and never played in the major leagues after 1947. Thompson batted .256 with the Browns, not enough to impress the team's manager, and he was also released. In 1949, however, Thompson went on to star with the New York Giants.

Bill Veeck early announced his intention of bringing African American stars to the Browns. And he made good immediately by signing the immortal Satchel Paige, who was certainly over the hill at age forty-five but still capable of pitching in the majors. Characterized as a cross between Socrates, Methuselah, and Dizzy Dean, the bubbly Paige went only 3–4 with the Browns in 1951, but the next year he was 12–10 with a 3.07 earned run average. Paige was also one of the all-time great crowd pleasers, and thousands came to watch him pitch.

Veeck immediately set about making Browns games interesting, even if the team was not competitive. The possibility of some surprise stunt, he hoped, would lure fans to the ballpark. They never knew what he might try. During "Grandstand Manager's Day" on August 24, 1951, Veeck had several thousand spectators manage the game. They were handed a placard with a green "yes" on one side and a red "no" on the other as they entered the ballpark. During the game, Browns publicity director Bob Fischel held up cards with proposed moves—steal, change pitchers, and the like—to which the grandstand managers flashed their opinions. All the while the Browns' regular manager, Zack Taylor, puffed a pipe while sitting in a rocking chair on the sidelines. The crowd changed the starting lineup, moved players to different positions, and altered the batting order. The fans loved it. They also did well in the game; the Browns won 5–3 to end a four-game losing streak.

The most outrageous stunt Veeck ever tried—the one for which he will always be remembered—took place in St. Louis on August 19, 1951. It was a hot and muggy Sunday afternoon in St. Louis, the kind that presses on one's senses, and the Tigers were in town for a double-header. The Browns had 20,299 in attendance, their largest crowd since 1947. After the first game Veeck had a large birthday cake rolled onto the infield, and the public address announcer informed the crowd, "Ladies and gentlemen, as a special birthday gift to manager Zack Taylor, the management is presenting him with a brand-new Brownie." Then out of the cake popped three-foot seven-inch Eddie Gaedel wearing a tiny Browns uniform with the number "1/8" on the back. Veeck had hired Gaedel from a talent agency for one hundred dollars for a single appearance at the game.

After the Tigers failed to score in the top half of the first inning, Gaedel went to the on-deck circle and took several menacing swings with a trio of pint-sized bats. As the umpire yelled, "batter up," manager Taylor scratched starting center fielder Frank Saucier from the lineup and inserted Gaedel as a pinch hitter. The Tigers protested, but the Browns produced a legitimate major-league contract

Eddie Gaedel, the shortest player in the history of major-league baseball, had a career consisting of one plate appearance for the Browns on August 19, 1951. He walked on four pitches. The stunt caused such an uproar that it was nearly expunged from the record books. Gaedel was paid one hundred dollars by Bill Veeck, who according to legend threatened him with immediate death if he did anything more than look at a pitch. Courtesy of the Missouri Historical Society, St. Louis.

Eddie Gaedel on the Browns' bench on August 19, 1951. Courtesy of the Missouri Historical Society, St. Louis.

and the umpire signaled that Tigers pitcher Bob "Sugar" Cain had to pitch to him. Gaedel had been warned not to swing; one story circulated that Veeck had even told him that he had a sniper with a high-powered rifle in the stands who would shoot Gaedel if he did so. As Gaedel stepped into the batter's box, Cain and Tigers catcher Bob Swift strategized over how to pitch to him. Cain wanted to throw to him underhanded, but league rules prohibited that. Then Swift tried to lay prone behind the plate to get low enough to make a target that was within Gaedel's strike zone, but the umpire stopped that as well. Gaedel crouched as low as possible and waited for Cain's delivery. Cain, facing a strike zone of about three inches, walked Gaedel on four pitches. His first two pitches were serious, but missed badly. By then Cain was laughing so hard that he lobbed the next two in and let Gaedel take his base. Gaedel then left the game for a pinch runner. The Tigers, despite Gaedel's pass to first base, won the game 6–2. Afterwards, Bob Broeg from the *St. Louis Post-Dispatch* ran up to Gaedel, shook his hand, and gushed, "You are what I have always wanted to be, an ex-big leaguer." Gaedel went on to earn thousands of dollars on the talk show and endorsement circuit because of his big day as a Brownie.

The good-natured Bob Cain was an appropriately good sport throughout this stunt. Many other pitchers would have been angry, thinking that Veeck and the Browns were making fools of them. Sal Maglie, the New York Giants' pitching ace whose nickname was "the barber" because of all the close shaves he gave opposing hitters, would probably have thrown straight at Gaedel's head. Browns historian Bill Borst opined that had Gaedel faced a less gentlemanly pitcher than Bob Cain, he might just as well have brought "a tiny pick and shovel with him instead of a bat so that he could have dug his own grave before getting into the batters box."

The rest of the baseball establishment, which did not much like Veeck anyway, expressed outrage. The day after Gaedel's appearance, American League President Will Harridge ordered that Gaedel's contract be rescinded and any mention of his appearance be expunged from all record books. Veeck refused to allow this absurdity to rest, however, and argued for months with Harridge that Gaedel's plate appearance should be recorded as a legitimate statistic. The great Eddie Gaedel caper probably proved the undoing of Veeck as an American League owner. From that point on his fellow owners worked unabashedly to oust him, even refusing to allow him to move the franchise in 1953 when every economic indicator demanded it.

Instead, they forced Veeck to sell the Browns to another consortium who immediately moved the team to Baltimore. With the Browns mired in last place in 1953 and the Cardinals recently sold to the cash-rich Anheuser-Busch Brewing Company, Veeck decided that he had to get out. The Browns were again drawing dismally at the ticket office, and since Veeck knew he was selling the team he refused to put much money into promotions. Attendance, which had been fairly good in 1952—518,796 fans—dropped to 297,238 in 1953. One day a fan supposedly saw Veeck on the street and asked him what time the game was that afternoon. Veeck responded, "What time can you be there?"

In their last season in St. Louis the Browns again lost a hundred games and finished last in the American League for a record tenth time. In a fitting ending, they ran out of clean baseballs during the season's final game and had to substitute soiled, scuffed batting-practice balls. The Browns left St. Louis unheralded and unmissed. Upon its arrival in Baltimore the team changed its name to the Orioles—they wanted to break with the losing tradition of the Browns—and reportedly burned the uniforms and other items with the Browns logo. In so doing, a legendary franchise passed into baseball history. It had taken more than fifty years, but the National League had finally won the war for St. Louis.

Low-Flying Cardinals

Although the Cardinals had been one of the best teams in the National League since the 1920s, in the late 1940s they entered a period of decline. Under Branch Rickey's leadership the Cardinals had benefited from an aggressive farm system that produced great talent, and they also had managed to make key personnel acquisitions that energized the team at key times. But in 1942 Rickey departed St. Louis to become general manager of the Brooklyn Dodgers, and his successors were not as successful in sustaining the Cardinals dynasty. Instead, Rickey built the Dodgers into the most dominant team in the National League. Between 1942 and their departure from Brooklyn after the 1956 season, Rickey's Dodgers won one World Series and six league pennants, finished second three times, and placed third twice.

The Cardinals were still a good team in the late 1940s, often finishing second to the Brooklyn "Bums," but they won no pennants. Part of the problem was the famously tight wallet of Cardinals owner Sam Breadon. He had an unwritten but well-known rule that the team would pay no player more than $13,500 per year. The only exception was shortstop Marty Marion, whom Breadon favored with $15,000. Routinely, when a player approached the $13,500 threshold Breadon had him traded to another team. In 1945 when the brother battery of pitcher Mort Cooper and catcher Walker Cooper demanded salaries as high as Marion's, Breadon had them shipped elsewhere. Mort Cooper went to the Boston Braves for another player and $60,000 in cash, and Breadon dealt Walker Cooper to the New York Giants for the then-unheard-of price of $175,000. The sums suggested the true worth of the two players. Both went on to star on pennant winners for their new teams.

Also to save money, Breadon allowed the Rickey-built farm system, once the best in the league, to wither. Each year the team of stars that had won four pennants and three World Championships between 1942 and 1946 got older. Each year Cardinals' stars asked for salary increases and found themselves being shipped off to other locales. Each year the team looked to its farm system for new talent and found the cupboard bare. So difficult did the situation become that Breadon decided to get out of the business and in 1947 sold out to a local consortium headed by Fred M. Saigh.

The Cards managed to make a final run at a pennant in 1949, running neck-and-neck with the Dodgers all season long. Up two games with five left to play, the Cardinals self-destructed and allowed the Dodgers to take the flag. On the way back to St. Louis after the season's final game, *Post-Dispatch* sportswriter Bob Broeg asked Cardinals manager Eddie Dyer when the team would next win a championship. In a moment of reflection Dyer said it would not be for a long time.

While the era of championship baseball seemed to be gone from St. Louis, one constant remained for the once-proud Cardinals. Stan Musial led the league in hitting several times during this period, and he became the strongest draw for the team. In 1948 "The Man" won his third Most Valuable Player award and led the National League in almost every batting category, including the batting race itself, which he captured with a .376 average. In 1950, 1951, 1952, and 1957 he also led the league with .346, .355, .336, and .351 batting averages respectively. He became the only player in major-league history to finish his career in the top fifty in all four hits categories: singles, doubles, triples, and home runs.

The Cardinals' failure to integrate contributed to the team's downfall as well. In addition to their excellent core of white players such as Duke Snider, Gil Hodges, Pee Wee Reese, Pete Reiser, and the like, the Dodgers had former Negro Leaguers Jackie Robinson and Roy Campanella, who solidified the Brooklyn dynasty of the late 1940s and 1950s. The New York Giants also built an outstanding team in the 1950s around black stars such as Willie Mays and Monte Irvin. In contrast to team owners such as Bill Veeck and the Dodgers' Walter O'Malley, new Cardinals owner Fred Saigh opposed any integration of the sport. His comment to *Ebony* magazine that he was only "interested in securing baseball players that might have capabilities of ultimately playing with the St. Louis Cardinals" was a veiled statement of his belief that African Americans did not possess the intelligence necessary to play in the major leagues. The Cardinals, therefore, missed out on recruiting many of the best players during the late 1940s and early 1950s.

As the city farthest south in the National League, St. Louis engaged in apartheid both as a matter of law and of practice. In that sense Saigh faithfully represented most of the population of St. Louis. For years after Jackie Robinson broke the color barrier, black players could not stay at their team's hotel or eat with teammates during road trips to the city because of ordinances segregating hotels and restaurants. Saigh and the Cardinals really did not care that this was the case and took no action to change it. Only in the late 1950s did Jim Crow restrictions finally begin to erode in St. Louis, no thanks to the efforts of the Cardinals' brass.

Indeed, during the Cardinals' first road trip to Brooklyn after Robinson began playing, in early May 1947, rumors circulated that they would refuse to play the game if Robinson walked onto the field. Supposedly North Carolinian Enos Slaughter whipped up this strike, reminiscent of the one staged in the 1880s by Cap Anson, but other Cardinals players probably supported him. One who did not, to his credit, was Stan Musial, although Musial was not a civil rights activist either. When word of the boycott reached National League President Ford Frick, he issued an ultimatum: "I do not care if half the league strikes. Those who do it will encounter quick retribution. They will be suspended and I don't care if it wrecks the National League for five years. This is the United States of America, and one citizen has as much right to play as another." On the day of the game the Cardinals took the field without protest.

When the Dodgers came to St. Louis on May 20, 1947, during their first swing west, there were no threats of a strike. The first game with the Dodgers turned out to be the largest weekday crowd of the season—16,249—mostly because the African American community turned out in droves to see Jackie Robinson play. They continued to attend games whenever Robinson was in town thereafter. "In Jim Crowish St. Louis," reported one periodical, "the Robinson rooting section was more noticeable. Their adulation embarrassed Robbie, made it harder for him to act like just another ballplayer."

Saigh successfully forestalled integration of the Cardinals throughout his ownership. When he sold out in 1953 to August A. Busch Jr., however, Busch immediately told the front office to search for Negro Leagues talent. When Enos Slaughter protested, Busch traded him to one of the whitest teams left, the New York Yankees. Busch also hired Quincy Trouppe, a former Negro League great, as a scout, and Trouppe signed several black players. In 1954 a trio of blacks made the Cardinals, integrating the team without incident. Two of them, pitcher Bill Greason and first baseman Tom Alston, did not make much of an impact. Greason played only one season, while Alston played for four. But pitcher Brooks Lawrence went 15–6 for the Cardinals in 1954. He did not do as well in 1955, but when traded to Cincinnati the following season he quickly became the ace of the Reds' pitching staff.

The Cardinals sank in the standings during the mid-1950s, finishing seventh in 1955, losing more games during the year than any Cardinals team since 1919, and closing out the season a dismal 30 1/2 games behind the pennant-winning Dodgers. They clearly had to rebuild. And rebuild they did.

When Busch purchased the team in 1953 for $3.75 million, he wanted a winner and he wanted it fast. "Gussie" Busch was one of the most interesting of all of the fascinating characters who pop up in major-league baseball. In buying the team, Busch wanted to use the Cardinals sports franchise to sell his premier beer, Budweiser. Busch was on the verge of taking his regional brewery to a national market, and the Cardinals were a key to his strategy for doing so. His beer would be advertised extensively during all Cardinals broadcasts, and it would be the only beer available at the team's home games. He would use the team the same way he used his Clydesdale horse teams, to help sell his beer to an ever-widening market. Soon after buying the Cardinals he also purchased their dilapidated playing field, Sportsman's Park, from the Browns. He tried to rename it Budweiser Stadium, but his underlings convinced him that it was an inappropriate name for a place where people took their children. Instead, they recommended Busch Stadium, which would advertise not only the beer but also the owner, in the same way that the field of Cubs owner Phil Wrigley advertised both Wrigley and his spearmint gum.

Ever a sparkling personality, Busch also loved being in the limelight, which was ensured by owning the Cardinals. As the head of a Fortune 500 company he might have money and power and a name that people in business circles recognized, but he was not a celebrity. That changed when he purchased the team. Suddenly, because of his Cardinal connection, when he called a press conference reporters and the public showed up to hear what he had to say. They recognized him on the street after seeing his face in the sports section, and he received the attention usually reserved for movie stars and national politicians. For the first time in his life, people coveted his friendship. It would be an understatement to say that he enjoyed the attention.

Busch was both an insecure and impatient man. His celebrity brought numerous opportunities for people to tell him how bad the Cardinals were and how he had to turn the team around. He took these criticisms to heart and sought desperately to guarantee success. As an outstanding businessman, Busch also thought he knew how to accomplish this task: hire the right people and let them do their jobs. He was willing to pay whatever was necessary to lure them to the Cardinals. After all, he had done the same thing with his brewery many times in the past. One anecdote demonstrates the naïveté of Busch in thinking this approach would work in major-league baseball. Soon after buying the team, Busch asked his manager which he needed worse, a third baseman or a first baseman. He told Busch he needed a first baseman. Busch then asked him who was the best and learned that Gil Hodges from the Dodgers was the best first baseman in the business. Busch then audaciously went to Walter O'Malley and offered to buy Hodges. O'Malley told him the price would be six hundred thousand dollars, and even if Busch had it, he still would not sell Hodges to the Cardinals. Busch returned to St. Louis muttering to himself about the irrationality of his fellow owners. He failed to realize that O'Malley's well-run Dodger franchise needed six hundred thousand dollars not at all, but required a stellar first baseman as much as did the Cardinals.

Instead, Busch hired Frank Lane as general manager and gave him license to build a pennant winner in St. Louis. Known to everyone as "Trader Lane" because of his penchant for making deals, Lane began wheeling and dealing like it was an addiction. And perhaps it was, for Lane could not contain himself from tinkering with the players on the roster. Among the most significant of his trades, in 1956 Lane traded future Hall of Fame second baseman Red Schoendienst, a cherished link to the glorious teams of the 1940s, to the Giants for Alvin Dark. He then tried to deal St. Louis icon Stan Musial to the Philadelphia Phillies for pitcher Robin Roberts. Only when word of this proposed deal leaked to the public, and the rumored trade was uniformly condemned, did Busch intervene. Busch, after a few too many drinks, then criticized Lane at a St. Louis sports dinner, and the two entered extended warfare. When Lane demanded a three-year extension on his contract, Busch sent him a telegram saying, "KISS MY ASS."

From that point forward, Lane's days with the Cardinals were numbered. In 1957 Busch replaced him with Bing Devine. Devine had at one time or another done virtually every job in the Cardinal organization, starting as an office boy when Branch Rickey was still running the team. Busch probably could have found no better person for the job. Devine knew the Cardinals inside and out. He had a sense of professionalism and honor. He knew talent when he saw it. He clearly understood the weaknesses of the Cardinals that needed to be shored up. He never let the trading bug get to him, but he was not afraid to make deals and he usually got the better end of them.

Most important, Devine had a vision of the kind of team he wanted to put on the field: the kind that had always won championships for the Cardinals in the twenty years between 1926 and 1946. Devine would build the Cardinals on solid pitching, excellent speed, and outstanding defense. Speed was important, Devine believed, because it helped both on defense and offense. He did not care too much for power hitting, believing that most home run hitters were not speedy and many were liabilities in the field. Certainly there were exceptions, but players with the all-around abilities of Willie Mays, Hank Aaron, and Mickey Mantle were extraordinarily rare. Instead, a player with the same type of skills as Stan Musial was ideal. Musial could hit home runs, certainly, but that was not his forte. He had great foot speed in his early years, an exceptional glove, and a terrific hitting eye. Devine certainly understood, though, that a player as good as Musial came along only once in a generation.

Devine showed that he knew how to build that ideal Cardinals team. He recognized that Ken Boyer, a player Trader Lane had brought up from the minor leagues in 1955, could be the cornerstone of a future pennant winner. Despite repeated entreaties from other teams to acquire Boyer's services from the Cardinals, Devine kept him, and Boyer proved for more than a decade to be both a stellar glove man at third base and an exceptionally capable hitter who had some power. In 1958 Devine acquired the team's first truly great black player in a trade with the Cincinnati Reds. Curt Flood patrolled the outfield for the next decade, until he was traded to the Philadelphia Phillies in 1969. Flood's refusal to accept that trade set in motion one of the most significant legal actions in baseball history, one that eventually broke down baseball's "reserve clause" and allowed players to act as free agents in seeking contracts with major-league teams.

In 1959 three more key players, pitcher Bob Gibson, first baseman Bill White, and catcher Tim McCarver, all joined the team. Gibson and White were African Americans. Gibson played seventeen years for the Cardinals, compiling a 251–174 lifetime record. One of the most intense baseball players ever to don a uniform, he dominated National League pitching throughout the 1960s, and eventually entered the Baseball Hall of Fame. White came over from the Giants and played seven outstanding seasons for the Cardinals. At the end of his playing career he became a broadcaster, and in 1989 he replaced A. Bartlett Giamatti as president of the National League. McCarver, a product of the team's minor-league system, soon took over as the regular catcher. He played on three pennant winners before going on to a career as a baseball broadcaster.

In 1960 the Cardinals acquired three more pivotal players who took over for the declining veterans of the 1950s. Julian Javier joined the team as the second baseman, while Ray Sadecki arrived to bolster the pitching staff. The Cardinals also acquired from the Philadelphia Phillies veteran pitcher Curt Simmons, who contributed several excellent seasons as a Cardinals starter. Outfielder Mike Shannon and shortstop Dal Maxvill joined the team in 1962, and veteran shortstop Dick Groat came over in a trade from the Pirates in 1963. The 1963 Cardinals had so many of the ingredients of a pennant winner in place that their entire infield—White at first, Javier at second, Groat at shortstop, and Boyer at third—started for the National League's All-Star team. But one last critical player was still needed. He came aboard in 1964 when the Cardinals traded with the Cubs for Lou Brock, a speedy outfielder who would bat lead-off for the Cardinals for the rest of his Hall of Fame career.

Kansas City, Here I Come (and Go)

After World War II the perennially excellent Kansas City Monarchs, leaders of black baseball, fell on hard times. In no small measure the integration of the major leagues brought about their demise, for the team's greatest stars quickly found their way to the National and American Leagues, thereby robbing the Monarchs of many of their box office attractions. An irony of the first magnitude existed here, for the ending of the baseball color barrier proved the undoing of the largely black-owned segregated teams. In October 1945 the Monarchs lost their first player to the white major leagues: Jackie Robinson, who was signed by Branch Rickey and the Dodgers. Robinson had played only part of the 1945 season with the Monarchs after mustering out of the army at the end of World War II.

Monarchs owners J. L. Wilkinson and Tom Baird, two white businessmen, did not object to baseball's integration, but they certainly opposed Rickey's methods of accomplishing it. Rickey failed to compensate the Monarchs for signing Robinson, claiming that the team did not have a valid contract with the player and therefore deserved no consideration. There had been nothing in writing, admittedly, but the Monarchs owners asserted a verbal contract. Robinson claimed such a contract did not exist. Rickey not only accepted Robinson's claim but also went further, arguing that there could not be a contract because the Negro Leagues were not a legitimate professional league, but "simply a booking agents' paradise. They are not leagues and have no right to expect organized baseball to respect them." Wilkinson and Baird thought about taking some action against Rickey, but decided that to do so would be viewed as an attempt to keep baseball segregated.

Instead, they began signing their star players to binding written contracts modeled on the standard major-league ones and took to selling players to the majors in much the same way that minor-league teams had done prior to the advent of the farm system. Over the next decade some of the finest players to make the transition from the Negro Leagues to the National and American Leagues came from the Monarchs. In 1947 Willard Brown and Hank Thompson left to join the St. Louis Browns. In 1948 Satchel Paige went from the Monarchs to the Indians. By 1955 Baird, who bought out the elderly Wilkinson in 1948, had sold thirty-eight players to major-league organizations, far more than any other Ne-gro League team. It was the only way to make ends meet in the declining Negro League. Among the departed Monarchs was eventual Hall of Famer Ernie Banks. So many players were sold to the majors in 1949 that Baird conceded the league championship series because he did not have enough players to field a team.

By 1955 the era of black baseball in Kansas City all but ended when the Phil-adelphia Athletics moved to the city and crowded out the Monarchs. Unable to compete with major-league baseball in his own backyard, Baird sold his team after the 1955 season. He later worked as a scout for the Kansas City Athletics. The Monarchs held on for a few more years before ceasing operations in 1960.

In place of the consistently excellent Monarchs, Kansas City now had the also-ran Athletics of the American League. The Athletics, owned by the staid Con-nie Mack, had enjoyed more than fifty years of roller-coaster operations in the "City of Brotherly Love." They had won nine American League pennants and five World Championships in Philadelphia—second only to the Yankees—but had also finished last in the league eight times. When new owner Arnold Johnson took over from Mack in 1954, he immediately announced that he was moving the team and promised to build a winner in western Missouri.

One humorous story about the Athletics' move to Kansas City involved the critical role of Chuck Roberts, Connie Mack's chauffeur in Philadelphia. Ac-cording to Ernie Mehl, a legendary *Kansas City Star* sports journalist, Roberts was pivotal in Mack's decision to sell the franchise to Johnson. After Mack and Johnson entered into negotiations, an upstart group of Philadelphians made its own offer to keep the team from leaving. The dueling interests only heightened the pressure on the ninety-one-year-old Mack, who had managed the A's for half a century. The bedridden Mack invited both bidders to his home on November 4, 1954, and vowed to make a decision regarding the sale of his shares.

Johnson arrived early and wound up in a discussion with Mack's driver out-side. Roberts already had taken a liking to Johnson and was interested in seeing the controversy settled, for the sake of his frail boss. He led Johnson into Mack's bedroom an hour before the other bidders were to arrive. Accompanying John-son was his attorney, Frank Schilpp. Mack spoke with them and, in a move that startled Johnson, agreed to sell for $604,000. Johnson was unprepared. He had to borrow his lawyer's personal checkbook to close the deal before the competition arrived.

Regardless of how the transaction was sealed, the Athletics arrived in Kansas City for the 1955 season. In its final year in Philadelphia the team had finished in last place, with 103 losses. Kansas City would see more of the same. During the Athletics' thirteen-year sojourn in Missouri, the team would place as high as sixth in the league only once.

On April 12, 1955, however, the Athletics won their home opener against the Tigers, 6–2, and enjoyed a crowd of 32,147 in Municipal Stadium. The team consistently drew well that first year and ended the season with 1,393,054 paid attendance. In 1956 the Athletics drew almost as well, but they began to trail off thereafter. In large measure this was because of the dreadful teams on the field coupled with a decline from the city's initial excitement in attracting a big-league franchise.

Not that the Athletics were without talent; it was more that Johnson seemed to keep trading the most promising players to the Yankees just when they had matured enough to contribute to Kansas City's fortunes on the field. In return, Johnson received worn-out Yankee stars and youngsters who needed time to develop. Indeed, some critics have concluded that the Kansas City Athletics were in effect a farm team for the New York Yankees during the late 1950s. In 1957, for example, the Yankees sent pitcher Ralph Terry to the Athletics and then two years later got him back in a second trade. With his seasoning in Kansas City, Terry

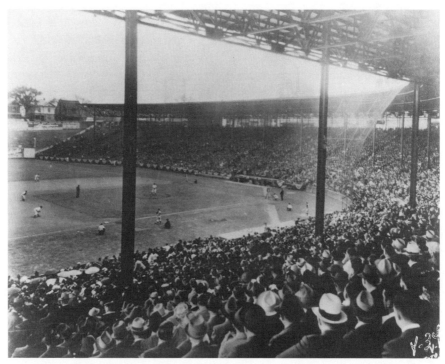

The Kansas City Athletics in action at Muehlebach Municipal Stadium. Courtesy of Special Collections, Kansas City Public Library.

had become ready to help the Yankees win five straight pennants between 1960 and 1964. Enos Slaughter did not fit into Yankee plans in 1955, so off he went to Kansas City for a year, and then right back to the Yankees in time to play on three pennant winners. Most famously, the Athletics sent slugging outfielder Roger Maris to the Yankees in 1960, just in time for him to break Babe Ruth's single-season home run record with sixty-one round-trippers in 1961. In all, Johnson made sixteen trades with the Yankees in five years, involving sixty-seven players. In almost every case, the Athletics got the worst end of the deal. Some thought that Arnold Johnson wore pinstriped underwear. The Athletics' first manager in Kansas City, Lou Boudreau, believed that Johnson owed the Yankee owner some great favor, perhaps for making it possible for him to purchase the team.

Just before the beginning of the 1960 season Arnold Johnson suffered a fatal heart attack. His heirs ran the Athletics for that season, but then sold out to Charles O. Finley in December. Finley was truly one of the most colorful, innovative, and unlikable persons ever to own a baseball team. He made George Steinbrenner, the arrogant owner of the Yankees, look like a model of decorum. Some said the "O" in Finley's name stood for "outrageous," and they were not far off. Finley said it stood for "owner." A self-made millionaire, Finley had gotten himself out of the steel mills of Gary, Indiana, through hard work, perseverance, and sacrifice. He was brash, profane, and overbearing, possessing all of the delicacy of a wrecking ball.

He wore out his welcome with the other members of baseball's elite community of owners even before he entered their ranks. They did everything they could to keep him from buying the team, but through sleight of hand and wooing of the Johnson heirs, Finley, displaying the snake-oil sales charm that had made him a millionaire, proved too fast for the snobbish owners. Their disdain for him only grew stronger with time, but Finley accepted it as his fate in life. He steamrolled his employees as well on a regular basis. In twenty-one years as owner of the Athletics he went through nineteen managers (three of them twice), more than thirty coaches, and dozens of office employees and broadcasters. He was notoriously cheap, engaging in exceptionally public and enormously petty arguments with players over salaries. At the same time, he could sometimes be outrageously generous. He would haggle in the most desperate manner with a player over a thousand dollars and then turn around and reward another with a twenty-five-thousand-dollar bonus. Wherever Finley went he engendered contempt, or so it seemed, and he never seemed to mellow with age. In Kansas City in 1961 many people thought him a jerk. In 1982, when he finally sold his team in Oakland, many people still thought him a jerk.

Finley was full of ideas, and he wanted everyone to hear them and to embrace them and feuded with those who dismissed them. With the Athletics in Kansas

Charles O. Finley with "Charlie O.," the Kansas City Athletics mascot loved by few people other than Finley himself. Some members of the team opined that their owner treated his Missouri mule better than he did his players. Courtesy of the Oakland Athletics Baseball Company.

City, he scrapped the standard-issue home white and road gray flannels in favor of colorful uniforms for his players. Clothed in Finley's favorite colors of Kelly Green and Fort Knox Gold, the Athletics were the subject of ridicule for years. Only in the 1970s did most of the other major-league teams adopt colorful and unusual uniforms. Finley also dressed young women on his ground crew in skimpy costumes. He instituted a mechanical rabbit, complete with a little Athletics uniform, to carry balls to the umpire during the game. He set up picnic tables beyond the outfield for fans to come and have supper. He placed lights in the dugout so that the fans could see what the team did there. He adopted several ideas from Bill Veeck, including an exploding scoreboard that launched fireworks whenever a Kansas City player hit a home run. Veeck once quipped, "If I ever run out of ideas, Charlie Finley will be out of business."

While in Kansas City Finley combed the countryside for the quintessential "Missouri Mule" and made it the team mascot. Named "Charley O.," the mule appeared in the outfield, in the dugout, and sometimes with team members riding it. It seemed to turn up whenever and wherever Finley wanted to see it. Some of the Athletics players thought that Finley treated "Charley O." better than he treated his employees. But they were wrong. Finley treated them exactly as he treated the mule, for he was domineering and paternalistic at the same time with all in his domain.

Finley also argued for the adoption of several substantive changes to the game. He wanted to use a yellow or orange ball because he believed the fans could see it more clearly. He advocated league realignment to take advantage of geographical rivalries. He thought the game should be speeded up and supported a three-ball walk rule. The other owners reluctantly agreed to a few of his ideas. They adopted his plan to play the All-Star Game and the World Series at night, during prime time, so it would have a greater television audience. He also pushed for the "designated hitter" rule to create more offense for the game, and in 1971 the American League accepted it.

Although Finley never saw success in Kansas City, while there he signed several players who would contribute to an A's dynasty in Oakland in the early 1970s. These included a North Carolina right-hander named Jim Hunter, whom Finley dubbed "Catfish," because he thought interesting nicknames attracted fan attention. Hunter debuted in Kansas City in 1965 and set about putting together a Hall of Fame career that included 224 victories and 166 defeats. Finley also signed Bert Campaneris, Dick Green, Rick Monday, Sal Bando, Blue Moon Odom, Chuck Dobson, and Hall of Famer Reggie Jackson during his sojourn in Kansas City.

Lack of success on the field in Kansas City translated into declining revenues as fewer people turned out to see the hapless Athletics. Finley was always duplicitous about his commitment to the city. Rumors circulated every year that Finley was moving the team, first to Dallas, then to Seattle, then to San Diego, then to "who knows where." Finley always publicly denied these rumors, announcing his loyalty to Kansas City and to Missouri. All the while he was negotiating to move the team first to Dallas, then to Seattle, then to San Diego, then to "who knows where." He only stayed in Kansas City because every time he went to the league for approval to move the Athletics the other owners opposed it; the vote was always 9–1.

By 1966 it had become clear that the days of the Athletics in Kansas City were numbered. The antics of the A's on the field and Finley off the field had soured Kansas City fans, and they collectively found other things to do during

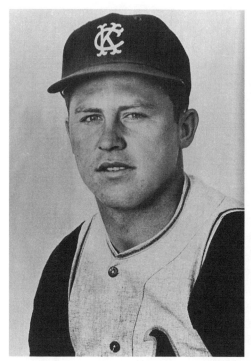

Jim "Catfish" Hunter began his major-league career in Kansas City, but did not reach stardom until after the Athletics had moved to Oakland. Other such players included Reggie Jackson, Bert Campaneris, and Sal Bando—all cornerstones for the Oakland dynasty of the early 1970s. Courtesy of the Oakland Athletics Baseball Company.

the summer. At the end of the 1967 season the team moved to Oakland. While the residents of Kansas City wanted, and deserved, major-league baseball, few mourned the loss of Finley's Athletics. Missouri Senator Stuart Symington summed up the position of most Missourians on the team's move: "Oakland is the luckiest city since Hiroshima." Symington then set out to ensure that major-league baseball returned to Kansas City by brokering a deal to place an American League expansion team in the city beginning with the 1969 season. Accordingly, the Royals came to town.

In the period between the late 1940s and the mid-1960s, major-league baseball in the state of Missouri was fundamentally changed. The Cardinals' pennant-winning machine collapsed, although the team then began a successful rebuilding process. The Browns departed St. Louis for good. The Monarchs ceased to exist. Finally, the Athletics came and went from Kansas City, causing a stir and leaving a bad taste. All of this set the stage for an enormously exciting era during the 1960s and 1970s.

The Swinging Sixties

In the spring of 1964 the St. Louis Cardinals were on the verge of returning to the greatness the team had enjoyed in the 1940s. The long dry spell was over. Between 1964 and 1968 the Cards would win three National League pennants and two World Series. In September 1963 Stan Musial, the greatest of all Cardinals players, retired in a bittersweet farewell at the old Busch Stadium. The next year the Cardinals won the National League pennant and then defeated the New York Yankees in the World Series. In 1967 the team took another championship over the Boston Red Sox, and in 1968 it earned a third pennant but lost to the Detroit Tigers in a dramatic seven-game World Series. These events, coupled with Curt Flood's landmark legal case against baseball's reserve clause, will make up the bulk of this chapter. Of course, at the end of the decade the Kansas City Royals began operations as well.

Return to Greatness

The 1964 edition of the St. Louis Cardinals included two future Hall of Famers—left fielder Lou Brock and pitcher Bob Gibson—and two other players who may yet be enshrined in Cooperstown—Ken Boyer and Curt Flood. These players led the Cardinals to their first pennant in eighteen years. Gone, unfortunately, was Stan Musial, who retired at the end of the 1963 season. It would have been a wonderful capstone to a marvelous career had Musial been able to play one more year and win one more championship. As it was, he remained in St. Louis to pursue business interests and to cheer his former teammates.

Hall of Fame Cardinals Pitchers of the 1960s

Player	Career Wins	Career Losses	Career ERA	Years With Cardinals
Steve Carlton	329	244	3.22	1965–1971
Bob Gibson	251	174	2.91	1959–1975

Hall of Fame Cardinals Position Players of the 1960s

Player	Career Batting Average	Career RBIs	Career Home Runs	Years with Cardinals
Lou Brock	.293	900	149	1964–1979
Orlando Cepeda	.297	1,365	379	1966–1968
Stan Musial	.331	1,951	475	1942–1963

The team also possessed a superb supporting cast. Tim McCarver, already making a name for himself as a keen observer of the game and the world, had taken over the regular catching duties the year before and was quickly proving himself a capable handler of pitchers and a competent hitter. Bill White, an intense and thoughtful player obtained from the San Francisco Giants in 1959, anchored the infield at first base. In 1964 he was in the last year of a three-year rampage, during which he batted more than .300, socked more than 20 round-trippers, and drove in more than 100 runs each season. He also regularly won the Gold Glove award as the National League's best fielder at his position. Julian Javier and Dick Groat nailed down the middle of the infield, each contributing superb defense and solid offense.

Ken Boyer, arguably the best third baseman who has not been enshrined in the Hall of Fame, won the league's Most Valuable Player award, batting .295, belting 24 homers, and driving in a league-leading 119 runs. Although Boyer's counterpart on the Cubs, Ron Santo, is the third baseman most often mentioned as overlooked by the Hall of Fame, Boyer deserves serious and sustained consideration from the Hall's Veterans Committee. Boyer's and Santo's numbers are quite comparable. Each played in the major leagues for fifteen seasons. Santo had a lower lifetime batting average at .277, but more home runs with 342. Santo also had a few more RBIs at 1,331. Santo never received an MVP award, while Boyer earned one. Each received Gold Glove awards five times. Boyer led the 1964 Cardinals squad that crushed a Yankee dynasty—the Yankees would not recover for more than a decade—while Santo never played in the postseason. Indeed, and this alone should probably disqualify him from consideration in the Hall of Fame sweepstakes, Santo was part of one of the most famous "chokes" in baseball history. In 1969 his heavily favored Cubs team took a huge division lead into August and then lost it in spectacular fashion to one of the perennial doormats of the National League, the New York Mets. All said, Boyer deserves more consideration for the Hall of Fame.

<table>
<tr><th colspan="5">Near Miss Hall of Fame Cardinals Players of the 1960s</th></tr>
<tr><td>*Player*</td><td>*Career Batting Average*</td><td>*Career RBIs*</td><td>*Career Home Runs*</td><td>*Years with Cardinals*</td></tr>
<tr><td>Ken Boyer</td><td>.287</td><td>1,141</td><td>282</td><td>1955–1965</td></tr>
<tr><td>Curt Flood</td><td>.293</td><td>636</td><td>85</td><td>1958–1969</td></tr>
<tr><td>Roger Maris</td><td>.260</td><td>851</td><td>275</td><td>1967–1968</td></tr>
</table>

With what could only be considered a stellar infield, the most important need for the Cardinals at the beginning of the 1964 season was in the outfield. Even with the stabilizing presence of Curt Flood in center field, it was not until the acquisition of Lou Brock in midseason that the outfield began to gel. Brock, who had been scouted for Chicago by famed Negro Leaguer Buck O'Neil, had signed with the Cubs for thirty thousand dollars off the campus of Southern University in Baton Rouge, Louisiana, a traditionally black college that had a history of producing both fine athletes and scientists. Brock never quite fit in with Chicago, where he consistently was a .260 hitter during his two seasons as a Cubs regular in 1962 and 1963. Few envisioned the Hall of Fame career that would come once he went to the Cardinals. For one thing, Buck O'Neil believed Brock was far too intense and counseled him to let his superb reflexes and agility take over. The more relaxed atmosphere in the Cardinals' clubhouse aided Brock, and he responded in 1964 with the first of eight seasons in which he hit at least .300. It was the left-hander's speed, however, that enthralled his new team. Brock provided the base-stealing threat at the top of the batting order that was needed to jump-start the Cardinals' offense. In his nineteen seasons Brock would swipe 938 bases, a major-league record since broken by Rickey Henderson, and even provided some power from his lead-off spot by hitting the occasional homer.

Brock's partner in the outfield, Curt Flood, was no less important to the Cardinals, and is also deserving of a place at Cooperstown (circumstances have thus far dictated otherwise). Flood, the team's defensive anchor in center field, took seven Gold Glove awards between 1963 and 1969. He finished his fifteen-year big-league career with a lifetime batting average of .293, identical to Brock's, hitting better than .300 six times and topping 200 hits in a season twice. He drove in 636 runs in the course of his career and superbly augmented Brock's base-stealing exploits from his spot as the second man up in the batting order. Brock's avowed value at the top of the Cardinals order could be said to have been underwritten by Flood during the team's glory years in the 1960s.

The team's general manager, Bing Devine, had also assembled a first-rate pitching staff. Bob Gibson came into his own in the early 1960s as the most dominating Cardinals hurler since Dizzy Dean thirty years earlier. An asthmatic right-hander from Omaha, Nebraska, Gibson had been pressed to excel both in athletics and academics by his older brother, who taught him that he had to succeed not only for himself but also for his race. And succeed he did. No one matched Gibson's intensity and concentration on the diamond, and few matched his fastball. He considered every game a form of combat, every batter an enemy to be vanquished, and he had no compunction about knocking down hitters to demonstrate his dominance on the field. He was famous for throwing knockdown pitches to former Cardinals teammates, lest they somehow think they might be able to hit his pitches or have an edge with him because of past friendships.

Gibson intimidated everyone, recalled teammate Tim McCarver. "He intimidated his teammates. He intimidated his manager. He intimidated his pitching coach." But mostly he intimidated the opposition. As a batter stepped up to the plate Gibson stared in with a withering look of utter disdain and menace. He looked, and acted, as if he wanted to kill you. "Losing was not an option," Gibson recalled. "There was going to be a battle," he added, "so let's see who the best man is." On game days, Gibson recalled, he was not a nice person, always intent on the battle to come.

Gibson also suffered no nonsense at all from anyone, and let even his close friends know when he considered something done or said ridiculous. When McCarver would come out and remind him where the baserunners were and the number of outs in the inning, Gibson would lash out at him. "Shit," he said, "I knew where they were, I put them there." He sent McCarver back to his position.

Gibson knew that baseball was not a "life and death" activity, of course, that it was simply a game. Two aspects of the game lured him as nothing else, however. First, there was the money to be earned playing it. As one of the greatest players of his era, Gibson's annual salaries were at the top of the scale. In the early 1970s, before the free agency era, Gibson's salary topped $250,000 per year,

Bob Gibson, the greatest pitcher in Cardinals history, threw so hard that he fell off the mound after almost every pitch. His on-field demeanor was one of the most intimidating forces batters have ever encountered. Courtesy of the Baseball Hall of Fame Library, Cooperstown, New York.

unheard of at the time. Second, he loved the competition. When he went to the mound the result was always a duel, with every pitch a thrust-and-parry in single combat.

At the same time, Bob Gibson was an enormously friendly and funny teammate in the clubhouse. His practical jokes kept his fellow Cardinals laughing. His kangaroo courts humorously disciplined players for failings on the field.

His leadership, in all its capacities ranging from stunning artistry on the mound to clubhouse pranks, served to help build the Cardinals into a cohesive, winning team. Cardinals manager Johnny Keane, who had managed Gibson in the minors, never doubted the greatness of this tall right-hander. He put Gibson in the rotation as soon as he arrived to take the skipper's job at midseason in 1961. Gibson immediately took on the role of the stopper in the starting rotation. He won eighteen games in 1963, nineteen in 1964, and then twenty or more in five of the next six seasons. In the process he became the greatest pitcher of the decade, an era dominated by outstanding pitchers.

Ray Sadecki, Ernie Broglio, and Curt Simmons also proved to be capable pitchers for the Cardinals and turned in excellent performances in the early 1960s. Broglio came up to the Cardinals in 1959 with a wicked fastball, and then promptly went 21–9 in 1960 to help power the Cards to a third-place finish. After a couple of mediocre years, Broglio went 18–8 in 1963. These performances convinced many that Gibson and Broglio would be the standard-bearers of Cardinals pennant winners in the future. In mid-1964, however, the Cards sent Broglio to the Cubs for Lou Brock. While many questioned the trade at the time, thinking that the Cubs had skunked the Cards, in Chicago Broglio never matched his early success, and he was gone from baseball by 1967.

Sadecki, a left-handed wunderkind, made his Cardinals debut a few months before his twentieth birthday in 1960 and immediately made a name for himself both as an arrogant bonus baby and a talented fireballer. He went 14–10 in 1961 with the Cardinals and then won 20 games in 1964. That was a great year for Sadecki, but he never matched it again. Midway through the 1966 campaign, the Cardinals dealt him to the San Francisco Giants for Orlando Cepeda. Sadecki was expendable to the Cardinals because other young pitchers such as Nelson Briles, Ray Washburn, and Steve Carlton were just breaking into the majors. For their part, the Giants were able to deal Cepeda because Willie McCovey had first base nailed down in San Francisco. The trade turned out well for both teams, but Cepeda's addition to the Cards proved pivotal to the team's pennants in 1967 and 1968.

For Curt Simmons, coming over to the Cardinals from the Philadelphia Phillies in 1960 provided a new lease on baseball life. One of the famed "Whiz Kids" of 1950, Simmons had helped lead the Phillies to the pennant that year with a 17–8 record. He turned in several other solid performances throughout the 1950s, but when he came to the Cardinals he blossomed into the kind of benevolent mentor every team needs in developing its young and talented pitchers. He also pitched exceptionally well for the Cards in 1963 and 1964, ending those respective seasons with 15–9 and 18–9 records.

It looked as if all the ingredients for a great team were starting to come to-gether in the early 1960s. The Cardinals had all of the attributes of its successful teams of the past: excellent pitching, great defense, and speed. But something else was also critical to the Cardinals success in 1964, and that was the team's abil-ity to bridge the racial divide. Everyone who visited the Cardinals' locker room recognized that the atmosphere was different from that of other teams. The black, white, and Latino players seemed to have easier relationships than else-where. They seemed not merely to tolerate their teammates but to enjoy them. No question, many of the premier players on the team were African Americans in 1964, and they certainly helped set the tenor of the clubhouse. But south-erners such as Ken Boyer and Tim McCarver were also committed to successful integration and brought that perspective to the team as well. This relative racial harmony was significant, for the Cardinals stood in striking contrast to many other major-league teams.

One anecdote illustrates this issue. While major-league baseball may be gen-uinely proud of integrating the game in 1947, there was little follow-through, and many teams did not integrate until well into the 1950s. African American players were left on their own to deal with racial injustice while representing the team, and they did not attain leadership positions with teams until much later. Indeed, the sport is still not appropriately integrated at all levels.

Curt Flood told of going to the Cardinals' spring training camp in Florida in the late 1950s and being sent to stay at a boardinghouse in another town, instead of occupying the same hotel where his white teammates were housed. A sensitive and thoughtful man, Flood was hurt and angered by this situation, and when the opportunity presented itself, he said something about it. When Cardi-nals owner August A. Busch, Jr., saw Flood at the training camp and struck up a conversation, Flood let slip that the situation of the black players was not the best. Busch was genuinely surprised that the black players were not staying at the main hotel with the "rest of the guys" and promised to do something about it. He arranged to have use of a hotel in St. Petersburg where all the Cardinals could stay together with their families during spring training. Of course, the Cardinals general manager, the field manager, and any number of other team officials were aware of this problem and did not challenge the conventions of southern segregation. But Busch was both able and willing to do something about it.

In later years, players from other teams recalled visiting the Cardinals' hotel and finding cookouts taking place with entire families, black and white, together. Living together for several weeks during spring training may have broken down the barriers of prejudice more than any other action the Cardinals could have taken. This harmony contributed to the team's success on the field and its attraction for the fans.

A Near Miss in 1963

After years of failing to contend for a pennant, toward the end of the 1963 season the Cardinals demonstrated that they were a genuine threat to win the National League race. For one thing, Stan Musial, who had suffered through several lackluster seasons in the twilight of his career, desperately wanted to win, and his teammates wanted to help him do so. At a team picnic at Busch's mansion during an off day in August, Musial admitted that 1963 would be his last year. "I can't do enough defensively or on the bases any more," he said, "and hitting, I can't concentrate well enough. I'm doing what I never did—taking called third strikes." Musial added, "I'd like to go out once more with a winner. Our 1942 team was further behind. We still have a chance."

And the Cardinals did. They rallied in August, beginning one of the greatest streaks in Cardinals history. They won ten games, lost one, then won nine more. The winning streak propelled the Cardinals from seven games behind the Los Angeles Dodgers to just one game behind, and the Dodgers were coming to town for a three-game series. St. Louis fans turned out in force to watch the games that would decide the pennant. Unfortunately, the Dodgers swept the series. Successive losses by Broglio, Simmons, and Gibson dashed all hopes for 1963. Although the team won ninety-three games that year, the most wins since 1949, the Dodgers were a team of destiny in 1963. They won ninety-nine games, then went on to take the World Series from the Yankees in four straight victories.

The most significant event in Busch Stadium at the end of the 1963 season was Stan Musial's retirement ceremony. The Cardinals great went to home plate wearing his uniform for the last time, and sporting a Boy Scout neckerchief. Indeed, Musial was the quintessential Boy Scout throughout his career. Ford Frick, commissioner of the National League, suggested that when Musial entered the Hall of Fame the master of ceremonies should "list no records, but merely state, 'Here stands baseball's perfect warrior, here stands baseball's perfect knight.'" The citizens of St. Louis would have agreed, both then and now. Musial remained in St. Louis thereafter, essentially as its first citizen. His annual visits to the Cardinals' clubhouse have become famed for the heartwarming manner in which he greets each edition of the team. An exhibit in the Cardinals Museum, titled simply "Me and Stan," consists of photos of nearly every celebrity imaginable standing with "The Man." A running joke at the museum is that while many people cannot identify all of the famous people in the photos, everyone knows Stan.

Taking the Brass Ring—1964

Stan Musial has always been a gentleman, possessed of a certain earthy frankness. He displayed both when he opined, "The Cardinals' couldn't win in 1964 with me in left field." Perhaps not, but that year the team posted the same 93–69 record it had achieved in 1963 with Musial playing. Only this time, the record was good enough to win the pennant. The Dodgers slumped to fifth place, and the Cardinals emerged to take their spot at the top of the National League. But it was a hard climb, and the Cards very nearly did not make it. At the midseason All-Star break, the team was mired toward the bottom of the league with a 40–41 record, and the Philadelphia Phillies, a team usually in the second division, were flying high atop the standings.

General Manager Bing Devine then arranged the trade that changed the fate of the Cards, obtaining Lou Brock and two others from the Cubs for Broglio and two other players. Brock began to hit, and the rest of the team followed suit. Bill White overcame a shoulder injury to produce seventy runs batted in (RBIs) in the last eighty games. Even as the Cardinals began to win, August Busch finally gave up on Bing Devine and fired him in the middle of the season. The rumor was that manager Johnny Keane would also be gone as soon as the season was over. Busch even had an off-the-record meeting with Leo Durocher to discuss the manager position. Busch did not much like Keane, who had a certain air about him that turned off many people, and the players did not much like him either, with his irksome rules that seemed designed to offend both their intelligence and their sensibilities.

Nonetheless, the team played at a torrid .687 clip throughout the second half of the season and went 21–8 in September en route to the pennant. On August 24 the Cards were in fourth place, eleven games behind the Phillies. By September 2 they had cut the Phillies' lead to six and one-half games. Even with this surge, the Cardinals needed help. The Phillies responded with one of the great "chokes" in baseball history, losing ten games in a row to allow the Cardinals back into contention. In the book *Ball Four,* Jim Bouton wrote that just before the September swoon *Sports Illustrated* did a cover story on the "phenomenal" Phillies. The team was excited about the story and pulled out all the stops for the writer and photographer. It came out just as the ten-game losing streak began, and it was a hatchet job of the worst sort. It told of personal peccadilloes and clubhouse hijinks, generally characterizing the Phillies as a bunch of miscreants. The Phillies filed a libel suit against *Sports Illustrated,* but as Bouton noted in his story's punchline, they might have won except that a week before the case went to court one of the team members was arrested for attacking a woman.

The Phillies' woes may have been accentuated by the *Sports Illustrated* story, but it was generally a situation of their own making. When the smoke cleared, the Cardinals had taken the flag by a game over the Phillies and Cincinnati Reds. Lest anyone try to take away some Cardinals glory by pointing out the Phillies' collapse, Ken Boyer was always quick to say, "Hell, we won it just as much as they lost it."

The 1964 World Series marked the Cardinals' tenth appearance in the Fall Classic, and the fifth time they met the Yankees. The series opened in St. Louis, where the teams split the first two games. Game Three at Yankee Stadium went into the ninth inning with the score tied 1–1, but Yankees great Mickey Mantle parked one in the right-field stands and the game was over. The Cardinals evened the series the next day when Ken Boyer hit a grand slam in the top of the fifth inning to make the score 4–3. As Boyer rounded the bases, his younger brother Clete, who played third for New York, threw pebbles at his feet. The fifth game went into the tenth inning before Tim McCarver hit a three-run shot to make the score 5–2. Gibson went the distance to win the game, striking out thirteen Yankees. The teams then returned to St. Louis and the Yankees forced a seventh game by beating the Cardinals 8–3, with an eighth-inning grand slam by first baseman Joe Pepitone sealing the outcome. This set up a dramatic seventh game in which Bob Gibson came back to pitch on two days' rest. Brock and Boyer hit home runs to power the Cards to a 6–0 lead after five innings, but the Yankees

The World Champion St. Louis Cardinals of 1964. Courtesy of Classicphotos.com, Ely, Minnesota.

closed to within 7–5 before Gibson got the last out in the ninth. The victory gave the Cardinals their first world championship since 1946 and the seventh in the team's history. Immediately after the series, Johnny Keane announced that he was leaving the Cardinals to take the manager's job with the Yankees. He did so just as Busch was prepared to fire him. Keane presided over the demise of the Yankees during the rest of the 1960s. In his place, Red Schoendienst took the helm for the Cardinals, serving for more than twelve years as the team's field leader.

The match between the Cardinals and Yankees in 1964 had symbolic value in addition to anything else that might be said about it. It represented baseball's present, the Cardinals, against the Yankees and the traditions of the past. The Cardinals were a well-integrated team with excellent African American players, and they were a rising power in the National League. The Yankees had failed to integrate until the mid-1950s, and then only modestly so. Their first black player, St. Louis native Elston Howard, joined the team in 1955. The Yankees ballyhooed Howard's breaking of the color line on the team by saying that he was a true "gentleman," and thereby appropriate to wear Yankee pinstripes. One wit observed that this was so much nonsense; after all, since when did baseball players have to be "gentlemen"? The Yanks in 1964 were also a franchise on the verge of collapse, with aging stars and not much down on the farm to call up to the majors. Their best player, Mickey Mantle, was nearing the end of his Hall of Fame career, and his replacement in the outfield would be Bobby Murcer, a decent player but not someone who would carry on the tradition of Ruth-DiMaggio-Mantle. The Cardinals' victory symbolized the death of the old manner of baseball, and thereafter every championship team would have African American stars as a critical element to success.

"El Birdos"—1967–1968

With essentially the same players as the year before, the Cardinals fully expected to repeat as champions in 1965, but fell embarrassingly short with an 80–81 record, good enough only for seventh place in the National League. Some of the key players were getting old and their skills were starting to decline. It was time for a change. New general manager Bob Howsam sent thirty-four-year-old Ken Boyer to the New York Mets for two journeymen players, neither of whom did much to help the Cardinals. Then Howsam dealt Bill White, thirty-five-year-old Dick Groat, and reserve catcher Bob Uecker to the Phillies for three players who also did little to improve the Cardinals' fortunes. In two big trades Howsam had dispensed with three of his four All-Star infielders. While many have criticized these trades as yielding little for the Cardinals (the only legitimate criticism), it was time to rebuild the aging infield.

Howsam redeemed himself by trading pitcher Ray Sadecki in May 1966 for Orlando Cepeda of the San Francisco Giants. Cepeda had enjoyed some great seasons for the Giants, but a knee injury looked to have ended his career. The Cardinals' physicians checked him out, pronounced him sound, and the trade was completed. Cepeda wrote in his autobiography, *Baby Bull,* that he had heard throughout his career that a trade to the St. Louis Cardinals was a blessing. The Cardinals were known for stable leadership in the front office, equitable dealings with players, and a clubhouse conducive to bringing the best a player had to offer to the fore. Cepeda certainly found this true in his case, for he "received a warm reception from the beginning." Stan Musial, who was by 1966 an official in the front office, came down to the clubhouse to see Cepeda before his first game and tell him how happy everyone was to have him with the team. Cepeda then met with manager Schoendienst and was told that he would bat cleanup for the Cards.

Cepeda responded immediately. He hit .301 in 1966 and slammed 20 home runs. In 1967 Cepeda had a banner year, averaging .325, stroking 25 homers, and driving in a league-leading 111 runs. That spectacular showing earned the Giants' throwaway the league's Most Valuable Player award. To a very real extent the 1967 Cardinals were Cepeda's team, and "El Birdos" easily took the pennant, to a Latin beat. It was enough to make one forget about Bill White, who had owned first base in St. Louis for a half-dozen years.

In 1967 the Cardinals also acquired a player with perhaps more emotional baggage than any other in the major leagues, Roger Maris. A strong young slugger from North Dakota by way of the Kansas City Athletics, Maris had gone to the New York Yankees and promptly broken Babe Ruth's single-season home run record with 61 round-trippers in 1961. Breaking one of the most cherished records in baseball was feat enough, but doing so in the glare of New York's media spotlight was too much for the introverted Maris. Never comfortable with the public relations aspect of the game, Maris cringed from the media barrage and seemed to range between anger and frustration with all of the attention. After that record-breaking season a hand injury robbed Maris of much of his power. He was still a fine ballplayer, although no longer a superstar. The Cardinals, of course, did not need power hitting, and the leadership told him so. It was a team built on defense, pitching, and speed. Maris nailed down right field as no one had since Stan Musial. For the two seasons Maris played for the Cardinals, the pennant-winning years of 1967 and 1968, the outfield of Lou Brock in left, Curt Flood in center, and Maris in right was probably the best in the major leagues.

Two long-term Cardinals also came into their own to help the team win pennants in 1967 and 1968. The first was Dal Maxvill, a weak-hitting but strong-fielding shortstop, who replaced Dick Groat after his departure in 1965. Mike Shannon, who had been playing in the outfield, moved to third base after Ken Boyer's departure and provided solid defense after learning the new position.

By 1967 the Cardinals' pitching staff included Bob Gibson, by then the top pitcher in the National League, and a group of talented youngsters. The most talented was Steve Carlton, who is now in the Hall of Fame. The left-hander came up in 1965, throwing hard but wild. He found himself in 1967 and went 14–9, then 13–11 in 1968. Nelson Briles also turned in a good 14–5 record for the Cardinals in 1967, and an even better 19–11 season in 1968. One other pitcher made an especially important contribution to the 1967 team, Dick Hughes. In just three years in the major leagues, Hughes had a lifetime record of 20–9, but in 1967 he went 16–6 for the Cardinals and helped them immeasurably down the stretch. Gibson, Carlton, Briles, and a solid supporting cast of other pitchers ensured that the Cardinals never let the opposition score many runs.

When the 1967 season opened at the new Busch Stadium in St. Louis—a large, ugly multipurpose municipal facility near the Mississippi River that had replaced the old Busch Stadium, *née* Sportsman's Park—every fan realized that the Cardinals were the class of the National League. But the Cards stumbled out of the gate and instead ran neck-and-neck with the Cubs throughout the first half of the season. A real scare came on July 13, when Bob Gibson suffered a broken leg from a line drive off the bat of Pittsburgh's Roberto Clemente. Gibson missed the next six weeks of the season. On July 25 the Cards and Cubs were tied with identical 56–40 records, but then the Cardinals won eighteen of their next twenty games. They continued to tear up the opposition down the stretch and finished the regular season with a 101–60 record, ten and one-half games in front of the second-place Giants. Season attendance surpassed two million for the first time, with 2,090,145 paid admissions, a franchise record that lasted until 1982.

In the 1967 World Series, the Cardinals met the Boston Red Sox, a team that carried the high hopes and good wishes of all New England and much of the rest of the country. The Red Sox are perhaps the most exasperating team in major-league history. After dominating baseball in the 1910s, they sold their best player, Babe Ruth, to the New York Yankees in 1918. They have not won a World Series since, although they have had several near misses. Some blame the team's futility on the "Curse of the Bambino," a mythical penance for sending Ruth to New York, but more appropriately it could be blamed on the racism of the franchise. The Red Sox were the last team in the majors to integrate, waiting until 1959 to add their first black player, Pumpsie Green, to the roster. In the 1960s there were still no African American stars on the Red Sox. By 1967 the roster included only Reggie Smith, then in his first full season and not yet the great player he would become, equally green George Scott, also-ran Joe Foy, and aging Elston Howard, who was a year away from his final season. The Red Sox missed out on the tremendous infusion of talent from the Negro Leagues that had energized other major-league teams. The decision to forestall integration was emblematic of the front office's generally poor baseball sense in overseeing the fortunes of the team.

When the Red Sox won the American League pennant in 1967, they did so against all expectations. They had not won a pennant since 1946 and had been perennial cellar dwellers throughout the 1960s. Boston had finished the 1966 season in ninth place in the American League. But two Red Sox players stepped forward in 1967 to lead the team to what came to be called the "Impossible Dream" pennant. By far the most important was left fielder Carl Yastrzemski, successor to Ted Williams in the Boston outfield and a Hall of Fame player in his own right. "Yaz" almost magically dominated the American League that year, inspiring his teammates by winning the Triple Crown: he was first in the league in batting average (.326), home runs (44), and runs batted in (121). He fully deserved the MVP award bestowed on him. The other Sox leader was right-handed pitcher Jim Lonborg. Although his lifetime record would be just 157–137, Lonborg had a storybook season in 1967, compiling a record of 22–9. It was his only twenty-win season, but he certainly made the most of his one great year. After 1967 a sore arm would plague him, eventually ending his career.

Most Americans viewed the Red Sox as the underdogs in the World Series and probably rooted for them to beat the powerful Cardinals. In contrast to the Cardinals' dominance in the National League, the American League pennant race had gone down to the last day of the season, with the Detroit Tigers and Minnesota Twins finishing only one game back of Boston's 92–70 record. Many predicted the series would be a four-game sweep for the Cardinals.

What they got instead was an excellent seven-game confrontation, with melodrama, excitement, and great feats and gaffes of legendary magnitude. The World Series opened in Boston's ancient Fenway Park, a bandbox of asymmetrical angles with a thirty-seven-foot-high wall in left field that caused more bad plays than anyone cared to remember. Bob Gibson took the mound for the Cardinals against Boston's Jose Santiago for Game One; Jim Lonborg needed another day's rest after having pitched the pennant-clinching game on the last day of the season. The Red Sox had never come across the likes of Gibson, who mowed Boston down 2–1 in a complete-game appearance, striking out ten and giving up only a homer to Santiago. Lou Brock had four hits in four at-bats, stole two bases, and scored both of the Cardinals' runs on hits by Roger Maris.

The second game went to the Red Sox, with Lonborg defeating Dick Hughes 5–0. Lonborg pitched an overpowering one-hitter, allowing only a double by Julian Javier in the seventh inning, while Yastrzemski socked two homers and drove in four runs. The World Series then moved to St. Louis for the next three games. Needing three more wins, the Cardinals fully expected to finish off the Red Sox in Busch Stadium.

The plan seemed to be on track during Games Three and Four. Briles stopped the Sox 5–2 in the third game, and Gibson shut out Boston for a 6–0 victory in Game Four. Brock went wild on the bases during both games and provided much of the offense for those victories. In the fifth game, however, Lonborg came back strong to pitch a three-hitter, defeating Carlton 3–1. The Red Sox were down, but certainly not out. No matter; many Cards rooters believed the team would put the Red Sox away at Fenway in Game Six.

Manager Red Schoendienst used a record eight pitchers trying to win the game, but they all came up short. Dick Hughes gave up three consecutive homers to Yaz, Reggie Smith, and Rico Petrocelli in the bottom of the fourth. With the game tied 4–4 in the seventh inning, Boston scored four times to defeat the Cards. Brock singled twice, had three RBIs, scored twice, and stole a base in the losing cause.

This set up a dramatic seventh game, with the Cinderella Sox poised to win their first World Series since 1918. Could the Impossible Dream team weave one last miracle to beat the Cards? A lot of fans thought so, and with Lonborg on the mound and Yaz leading the offense, it seemed like there might just be one last great comeback in store to seal the legend of the 1967 Red Sox. But they had not bargained on Mr. Gibson. Lonborg against Gibson—what a duel! But Lonborg was pitching on two days' rest against a fully rested Gibson, and Gibson brought all of his intensity and menace to the game on that day.

In the end the game did not live up to its hype. Lonborg ran out of gas early and gave up two runs in the third, two more in the fifth, and finally three in the sixth on Javier's three-run homer. Gibson pitched a three-hitter, striking out ten and capping off his day by hitting a fifth-inning homer of his own. The Cardinals won, 7–2.

Gibson, Brock, and Maris all had a superb series. Gibson won three of the four Cards victories, with twenty-six strikeouts in twenty-seven innings and a tiny 1.00 earned run average. Indeed, counting 1964, Gibson was 5–0 in World Series competition. Brock had twelve hits for a .414 batting average, and Maris batted .385 with ten hits and seven RBIs. Flood, McCarver, and Cepeda all had a poor World Series at the plate, but played well enough in the field. Stan Musial, who had succeeded as general manager when Howsam left in 1966, took pride in the team's performance. While on top, he decided to leave the position at the end of 1967 to pursue a growing set of businesses in St. Louis. Bing Devine came back to lead the front office.

The "El Birdos" team of 1968 repeated easily as National League champions. With essentially the same personnel as the previous year, the Cards finished the season with a nine-game lead over the second-place Giants. The 1968 season was dominated by pitching—it is often referred to as "The Year of the Pitcher"—and no one was more dominating than Bob Gibson. His landmark year ended with a 22–9 record, which was impressive enough, but his 1.12 ERA, 268 strikeouts, 15 straight wins, and 13 shutouts were phenomenal. In June Gibson had a stupendous month, pitching five shutouts and compiling a forty-eight-inning streak during which he allowed no runs; in ninety-five innings he gave up only two runs. Not surprisingly, Gibson was named National League MVP and was unanimously chosen the Cy Young Award winner as the league's outstanding pitcher.

The 1968 edition of the Cardinals did not quite match their record of the previous year, finishing the season at 97–65. Many of the players also failed to match their previous performances. Batting averages declined precipitously, and only Curt Flood batted more than .300. Their World Series opponent would be much more difficult this time: an overpowering Detroit Tigers team that had gone 103–59 to run away with the American League pennant. Detroit's pitching staff was led by Denny McLain, who had gone 31–6 with a 1.96 ERA, but McLain was certainly far from the best pitcher in baseball that year and, as the World Series would show, may not even have been the best pitcher on the Tigers.

Not surprisingly, the first game in the series, which matched Gibson against McLain, was billed as a pitcher's duel. McLain pitched well into the fourth inning, but then the Cards scored two runs, and the Tigers' ace left the game in the fifth. Meanwhile, Gibson overpowered Detroit's vaunted offense, led by Al Kaline, Norm Cash, Willie Horton, and Bill Freehan, by striking out a record seventeen batters in the course of a complete-game victory. As a fourteen-year-old I recall arriving home from school in the eighth inning as Gibson was on the mound en route to perhaps the most dominating pitching performance in World Series history. His eyes seared the opposing batters as he stared in from the mound. His trademark long-sleeved red undershirt was soaked in sweat, and he literally fell off the mound with every pitch. Occasionally the television microphones picked up his grunts as he hurled the ball into McCarver's glove. In the ninth inning one could see Gibson visibly tiring, and he allowed a lead-off single to Mickey Stanley. With a player on first, however, by sheer force of will, Gibson struck out the heart of the Tiger order—Kaline, Cash, and Horton—to end the game. He won 4–0, and the Cards were one up in the series.

Game Two pitted the second-best pitcher on the Tiger staff, an overweight left-hander named Mickey Lolich who looked more like a butcher than a ballplayer, against the Cardinals' Nelson Briles. The Tigers pounded Briles while Lolich pitched masterfully, and Detroit won the game 8–1. The Cardinals came back in Game Three with a 7–3 victory to set up a rematch in Game Four between Gibson and McLain. The Cardinals disposed of the Detroit hurler early and Gibson pitched another complete game; the final score was 10–1. Lolich then beat Briles again in Game Five, and in the sixth game the Tigers pounded the Cards 13–1, with McLain winning against Ray Washburn.

Again, the Cards faced a seventh-game moment of truth. This time Gibson faced Lolich. There were no better pitchers anywhere, and for six innings they dueled to a scoreless tie. In the seventh, however, the Tigers scored in the most unlikely way. With runners on first and second, Jim Northrup lofted a fly ball to deep center field. Gold Glover Flood went back as he had done so many times before to make the putout, but this time he stumbled, allowing Northrup to hit a two-run triple. Northrup also scored a moment later, and the Tigers went on to a 4–1 victory. Gibson had lost his first World Series game, while Lolich had earned three Tiger victories and McLain the other. Lolich would later demonstrate both his superb talent and great longevity through sixteen years in the majors and two twenty-win seasons. Flood blamed himself for the loss, but then again so did Gibson, and McCarver, and Maris, and Cepeda, and Briles, and everyone else. It was a near miss for an outstanding Cardinals team. Unfortunately, it would be another fourteen years before they would have the opportunity to redeem themselves in the World Series.

The Curt Flood Case and the Beginnings of Free Agency

Current major-league ballplayers should genuflect when they see a photograph of Cardinals outfielder Curt Flood, for it was he who first challenged the right of his team's owner to trade him without his acquiescence. When the 1969 edition of the Cardinals slipped to fourth place in the National League East Division, it was time to make some personnel changes. Accordingly, Bing Devine traded Flood to the Philadelphia Phillies in October. But Flood, who considered Philadelphia a racist city, saw no reason to uproot his family from their comfortable existence in St. Louis. He also had other business interests in St. Louis and did not wish to end them. Flood resented hearing about the trade third-hand from a journalist rather than from the team's general manager. Finally, and perhaps most important, Flood firmly believed that he had given the Cardinals his best for twelve seasons, and that both human dignity and his hard work had earned for him the right to be a part of any decision that affected him so fundamentally. He refused to report to the Phillies and challenged the right of team owners to make decisions about their employees without their input.

Since the Cardinals no longer wanted him, Flood believed he should be given the right to pursue baseball contract talks with other teams. He set out to challenge Major League Baseball's "reserve clause," a seemingly inviolate section of all player's contracts that allowed the team the right to reserve the services of their players for the next season even without a signed contract. This clause extended back to 1876, when coal baron William A. Hulbert had set about ensuring that power resided with the owners rather than the players, and despite occasional challenges the players had never been able to overturn it. Since the reserve clause stated that the club had the right to renew a player's contract following each season, it made a player the property of the team that first acquired him for the remainder of his career. While the contract, and hence the player, could be traded, the player could not unilaterally choose to play for another team even if he did not have a current signed contract.

This effectively established a baseball plantation system. Despite the game's growing popularity and enormous new income from radio and television rights, the average player's salary stayed at almost exactly the same point—seven times the average of the general population's—as it had for a century. In the decade of the 1960s, as civil unrest and protests from many quarters arose, baseball players began to show greater disenchantment with this system. In 1966, Dodgers pitching stars Sandy Koufax and Don Drysdale decided to use an agent to negotiate their contracts in an effort to leverage their salaries. Dodgers owner Walter O'Malley refused to talk to the agent and summed up the owners' view. "Baseball," he stated, "is an old fashioned game with old fashioned traditions." Without any real power, the duo was forced to sign for salaries several times less than they had demanded.

These and other contract disputes precipitated a revitalization of the Major League Players Association, an organization that had existed on paper for some time. After the 1966 hiring of Marvin Miller, formerly Chief Economic Adviser to the United Steel Workers of America, the Association became a powerful force on behalf of the players. In Miller they had finally found a battle-tested leader in their fight against the reserve clause. "The moment we found out that the owners didn't want Marvin Miller," Flood recalled, "we knew he was our guy."

When Flood's difficulties arose in 1969, he wrote an eloquent and moving letter to baseball commissioner Bowie Kuhn stating his position. It read:

Dear Mr. Kuhn:
    After twelve years in the major leagues, I do not feel that I am a piece of property to be bought and sold irrespective of my wishes. I believe that any

system which produces that result violates my basic rights as a citizen and is inconsistent with the laws of the United States and of the several States.

It is my desire to play baseball in 1970, and I am capable of playing. I have received a contract offer from the Philadelphia club, but I believe I have the right to consider offers from other clubs before making any decisions. I, therefore, request that you make known to all Major League clubs my feelings in this matter, and advise them of my availability for the 1970 season.
Sincerely,
Curt Flood

Kuhn did not respond to the letter.

Flood then met with Miller and the leaders of the Players Association. Miller asked him pointedly, "Do you realize you might never play again?" "Will you accept a better contract to settle the case?" "Are you aware how much this could mean to future players?" Flood answered the questions automatically—"Yes," "No," "Yes." Board member Tom Haller, as Miller recalled in his autobiography, then said, "This is a period of black militance. Do you feel you're doing this as part of that movement? Because you're black?" The question caught Miller and several others by surprise, but Flood remained as calm as ever. "All the things you say are true," he agreed. "And I'd be lying if I told you that as a black man in baseball I hadn't gone through worse times than my teammates. I'll also say, yes, I think the change in black consciousness in recent years has made me more sensitive to injustice in every area of my life. But I want you to know that what I'm doing here I'm doing as a ballplayer, a major league ballplayer."

While Flood had never been active in the civil rights movement, his complaints against baseball had sprung not only from the reform-minded sixties but also from his personal experiences as a black man in a racist America and a particularly prejudiced baseball establishment. Flood recalled the taunts and indignities when he had played in the South and from white opponents. He reflected across the years that "they called me everything but a child of God." And for an especially sensitive and thoughtful man such as Flood, racist comments, even if unintended, cut deeply. He went on to say that he was pleased that God made his skin black, but he wished God had made it thicker. While Flood did not challenge the reserve clause in baseball as a black man, from the start of his career he and all other blacks remained baseball outsiders. From that vantage point, Flood decided to challenge the reserve clause.

Despite all the racism that Flood saw in the nation at large, it was no doubt racism in contract negotiations that most shaped his views on the reserve clause. After learning that a white player got a large raise when none came to him, he inquired about it to a Cardinals executive. Flood said he was told that it was necessary "because white people required more money to live than black people. That is why I wasn't going to get a raise." If playing baseball failed to live up to the tirelessly constructed dream Americans had made it to be, contract negotiations, thanks to the reserve clause, proved the most contentious episode in owner/player relations.

Although Flood pursued his fight against the reserve clause simply as "a baseball player," throughout the dispute no one in America forgot that he was a black baseball player. It was a time when Americans had an increasingly uneasy view of the Civil Rights campaign. While Martin Luther King, Jr., and his methods of nonviolent resistance had succeeded in raising the consciousness of most of America, many in the press condemned Flood as an "uppity black" seeking merely self-gain and caring little about tradition. The owners tried desperately to spread this view, especially Cardinals owner Gussie Busch, and most Americans felt quite comfortable in accepting it. Even with Flood's talk about principles and morality, much of America alternatively saw Flood as a selfish opportunist or the ignorant dupe of Marvin Miller. He was neither. With quiet dignity Flood challenged American's views on not only baseball but also race.

To some Americans long disenchanted with baseball, Flood's principled stand brought life back to the game. Writer Gerald Early described what Flood meant to him and many other young African Americans:

> In the sixties, I felt that baseball had lost some of its resonance for me, because these players did not seem to be in touch with what was going on. Everything was becoming very politicized, and this was particularly true for black players. . . . [To] the very argument that [older players] were going to give about the status quo . . . I said because it must be done, that we must be willing to show that we were willing to pay a price in order to be treated with dignity.

In giving up his baseball career and showing that he was willing to suffer, Flood followed the precedent that earlier black reformers had set. Yet in knocking down the stone walls of the mythic baseball castle and bringing the game back to real life, Flood broke the "national agreement" that had held for almost a century.

On January 16, 1970, Flood filed suit against Major League Baseball and its reserve clause for $3.75 million. His playing career went on hold while *Flood vs. Kuhn* debated the idea that the reserve clause violated the Thirteenth Amendment—which bars slavery and involuntary servitude—prevented a fair market system, and depressed wages. Baseball had faced legal challenges in the past, but never had a player of Flood's caliber attempted to assail the game's sacred clause. Furthermore, Flood had earned ninety thousand dollars per year, yet accused baseball of violating the Thirteenth Amendment that barred slavery and involuntary servitude. With a few exceptions, the public and the media initially reacted to Flood's action in utter disbelief, branding the outfielder an ingrate, a destroyer, even a blasphemer.

Flood's case eventually went to the Supreme Court. In oral arguments, Flood's lawyer, Arthur Goldberg, put forth strong evidence to show that baseball's reserve clause violated antitrust laws by depressing wages and limiting a player to one team. Baseball's defense team attempted to counter Goldberg's broad arguments for human and labor rights point by point, but the crux of baseball's argument dealt with such ideas as tradition and the "Good of the Game." When finally decided, the Supreme Court ruled in favor of baseball 5–3, not on the strength of their case, but on a strange perception that baseball simply should stay the way it was.

So Flood lost himself in art. Leaving baseball behind, he departed for Denmark to paint in Copenhagen. Washington Senators' owner Bob Short brought him back. In time for the 1971 season, Short negotiated an agreement with the league and the Phillies to acquire Flood. He also told Flood that he could leave the team at season's end, no questions asked. All parties agreed. While the case continued, Flood returned to the field. But the time off proved too long. In thirteen games, Flood batted .200. With his St. Louis photo studio collapsing in financial ruin, creditors suing him, and a subpoena for back alimony, Flood jumped the team on April 27, 1971, and flew to Spain.

While losing in court, Flood's cause would eventually change the face of professional baseball. Less than three years later, pitchers Dave McNally and Andy Messersmith took on the reserve clause. They played out the option year on their contracts and won free agency through binding arbitration. A new era had dawned. By the time of Flood's death in January 1997, the media almost uniformly heaped praise upon the former center fielder. The day following Flood's death, Senator Orrin Hatch of Utah introduced the "Curt Flood Act" in Congress, designed to strip baseball of its anti-trust exemption, saying, "The time has come to finish what Curt Flood so courageously began." At the turn of the twenty-first century, America stood more prepared to accept a complex and controversial leader such as Curt Flood. He had finally won.

The A's Are Dead, Long Live the Royals

While the St. Louis Cardinals demonstrated throughout the 1960s that they were one of the best teams in the National League, the cross-state Kansas City

Athletics merely disguised themselves as major-leaguers while the team served year after year as doormat to the rest of the American League. Not to be outdone, Athletics fans disguised themselves as empty seats at Municipal Stadium. This situation resulted from the antics of Athletics owner Charles O. Finley, whose capacity for double-dealing doomed the Athletics in Kansas City from almost the beginning. A few examples will suffice. When Finley first took over he announced a huge facelift to Municipal Stadium. That was well and good, and he announced that "you must spend money to make money." He made much of the half-million dollars he was putting into the city's dilapidated stadium. He installed light poles every fifty feet around the stadium to improve night access. He painted the exterior canary yellow, which few people liked, but it was better than the peeling paint that it replaced. Inside, he installed new field boxes painted citrus yellow, painted reserved seats and bleachers desert turquoise, painted the upright beams burnt orange, and painted the two vertical foul poles a most horrid fluorescent pink. "We may not have the best ballpark in baseball," he announced, "but we sure have the sexiest." Later he mercilessly pressed city officials for reimbursement for these "improvements" to the stadium.

More important, Finley proved deceitful in his dealings as a team owner. When the Athletics were for sale in 1960, city leaders worked hard to have a local consortium purchase it, to help ensure the team stayed in Kansas City. When no one was able to put together a deal, in stepped Finley, offering to purchase only 52 percent of the Athletics with the remaining 48 percent owned by local interests. This would hedge against any quick moves of the team out of the city. All the while Finley swore he would keep the team in Kansas City, despite sagging attendance and horrendous performances on the field. Within a few months, however, he told the minority owners that he had to own 80 percent of the team or forgo the full tax benefits, and they sold to him! Then only a few months later he demanded 100 percent ownership—always promising not to move the team, and even creating a corporation with locals on the board to help run it. He then proceeded to take all power away from that board.

This record of deceitfulness had most observers convinced by the mid-1960s that the Athletics would not remain in Kansas City for long. Then Finley pulled the final straw. We went looking for a place to move the Athletics, a place that would give him a new and luxurious stadium, an attractive incentive package, and a big tax break. And preferably, he wanted a place that was more exotic than heartland Kansas City. The word got out almost immediately as Finley made the rounds to other cities. The *Kansas City Star*'s Ernie Mehl broke the story. Finley denied it, saying, "I know nothing about the rumors. They're rather disgusting." Deliberate lies angered Mehl. He wrote, "Had the ownership made a deliberate attempt to sabotage a baseball organization, it could not have succeeded as well. . . . It is somewhat the sensation one has in walking through a hall of mirrors designed to distort, where nothing is normal, where everything appears to be out of focus. There has never been a baseball operation such as this, nothing so bizarre, so impossibly incongruous."

Finley claimed to have been libeled by Mehl, and announced that he would not stand by and let someone do that to him. "It makes me so sick it almost makes me want to take the club out of here," he said. But Finley did not stop by just setting up Mehl as the fall guy for plans to move the team. He also organized an "Ernie Mehl Appreciation Day" at the ballpark for the next Sunday afternoon. On that day a truck circled the stands with a Mehl impersonator writing nasty comments by dipping his pen in a well of poisoned ink. Mehl, a respected forty-year veteran of journalism in Kansas City, did not find the "tribute" either funny or flattering. He declined to attend. Ford Frick, the commissioner of baseball at the time, was shocked by Finley's antics. Frick asked the Associated Press to run a statement in which he said, "Such things do not belong in baseball and I called Mehl this morning to apologize to him both personally and in the name of baseball."

The episode was all the more disconcerting to baseball executives and Kansas City residents because of whom Finley had singled out for abuse. Born in 1900, Mehl had long been considered the godfather of sports in Kansas City, especially baseball. Mehl had gone to work for the *Star* in 1920 and was sports editor from 1950 until he retired in 1965. He worked for years to bring a major-league baseball franchise to the city. When A's owner Arnold Johnson died in 1960, Mehl was part of the group that tried to buy the team, and many were still upset that he had lost out to Finley. Mehl was also an ordained minister who appeared in many pulpits on Sunday mornings while traveling as a baseball writer and had built up goodwill everywhere. Finley did not seem to care about any of this and abused him repeatedly over the years. When Finley finally moved the A's to Oakland in 1968, Mehl led the effort to have the American League place an expansion team in Kansas City, and took great pride in the success of the Royals. He lived just long enough to see the Royals win the World Series in 1985, another source of great pride for the Kansas City stalwart.

Within three years of purchasing the Athletics, Finley publicly began trying to move the team elsewhere. He joked about taking it to Louisville: "We have these caps that have K.C. on the front, and we don't want to throw them away, so I think we'll call ourselves the Kentucky Colonels. And before every game, after 'The Star-Spangled Banner,' everyone will sing, 'Oh, the sun shines bright.' " The race was on to get out of Kansas City, and Finley would not rest until he had done so. Everyone else looked forward to Finley getting out of Kansas City as well, but they wanted him to leave the Athletics there when he left. Finley would have none of it.

Joe McGuff, who had by that time replaced Mehl as sports editor for the *Star,* wrote an open letter to the other owners in the American League in 1967 as they were preparing to decide on Finley's petition to move. In it he detailed what had taken place in Kansas City since Finley bought the Athletics:

> To sum up briefly: Finley purchased controlling interest in the A's in December, 1960. He made elaborate promises to leave the franchise here. By the following August he was attempting to move to Dallas–Fort Worth. On May 18, 1962, he made another attempt to move to Dallas. On September 19, 1962, he asked for a new stadium here. On September 20, 1962, he said the city was justified in being angry about his attempts to move but requested that he be given an opportunity to make a fresh start. On July 9, 1963, he made his first attempt to move to Oakland. Negotiations for a new lease on Kansas City's Municipal Stadium started in December, 1963. Finley promised he would operate here regardless of the outcome of the negotiations. On January 7, 1964, Finley signed a conditional lease in Louisville and announced plans to move the A's there. On January 16, the American League ordered Finley to sign a lease in Kansas City. Finley then asked for a new meeting for the purpose of requesting permission to move to Oakland. On February 29, Finley signed a lease here under threat of losing his club. He later instituted a suit against the city to have the lease voided in favor of a previous lease that he claimed was the only valid lease. In the meantime Finley's name was linked with possible franchise moves to Atlanta and Milwaukee. In the autumn of 1966 stories appeared about the possibility of the A's being moved to Oakland. . . . Finley did not comment on any of these stories. On May 7, 1967, stories appeared in the *New York Daily News* and the *New York Times* about the possibility of the A's being moved to Oakland. Finley, contacted by the Associated Press in Chicago, declined to comment. His unwillingness to comment . . . has created the definite impression here that he will attempt to move.

Finley's only comment about any of this at the time, and thereafter, was that the journalists in Kansas City were after him.

McGuff suggested that Finley had engaged in a deliberate pattern of lies and subterfuge in discussions over the status of the Athletics in Kansas City. It did not really matter. After years of lobbying the other owners, Finley finally had his way. On October 18, 1967, the American League owners met in Chicago to consider moving the Athletics to Oakland. On the first ballot he was short, but only by a few votes. One team, the Baltimore Orioles, voted against him, while three abstained. Frank Cashen of Baltimore gave this reason for voting no: "We didn't really believe that moving the team to Oakland was the answer to Charlie's problems. Very frankly, we felt the A's had not done the proper market studies to look at the various places that were available. And we thought it would certainly hurt the San Francisco Giants to put another team into the Bay area." On the second ballot on October 18, the Yankees changed their vote from an abstention to affirmative, and Finley got the green light to move. The rumor is that Finley had the moving vans at the stadium before sundown.

At the same meeting the owners voted to expand the league by no later than 1971. While the owners sat around congratulating themselves for their wise decisions, the Kansas City politicos got busy and brought the party to a crashing halt. A delegation led by Kansas City mayor Ilus Davis and Missouri Senator Stuart Symington weighed in to let them know that taking major-league baseball away from Kansas City could have dire consequences. Symington promised to hold hearings on baseball's management and assured the owners that he would not stop until he had stripped away the game's anti-trust exemption. Davis threatened a court injunction against moving the team.

American League President Joe Cronin, an old baseball hand but a naive political operator, was shaken by the threats. He reconvened the owners and put together a plan to expand the league in 1969, rather than 1971. He also gained approval from the owners that one of the expansion teams would be placed in Kansas City. Frank Cashen recalled:

> One thing I'll never understand is the events of that day. Voting in the morning to allow Finley to leave Kansas City. Then voting in the afternoon to expand into Kansas City because we considered it one of the hotbeds of baseball. As an American Leaguer, I have to say I think that was a disgraceful proposition to have occurred in one day. Expansion was forced, and I'm not sure at all that it was good for baseball—as far as comparing the caliber of the game before that expansion and now.

Not surprisingly, Cedric Tallis, general manager of the expansion Kansas City Royals, had a different take on the decision. "The American League never would have permitted Finley to move if they hadn't conceived of having an orderly expansion and another club in Kansas City. Expansion was a good thing at the time. We got the growing pains over quickly, and the hoppers are full. . . . All in all, I think it was best that the marriage between the A's and Kansas City was dissolved."

The American League and the Kansas City business community wasted no time in putting together a deal to birth the Royals in the Missouri heartland. In January 1968 Ewing Kauffman, a Kansas City resident and a self-made multimillionaire in pharmaceuticals, became owner of the new franchise. Kauffman's board of directors, a real board this time, included a number of Kansas City luminaries, among them Finley's old nemesis Ernie Mehl. Kauffman also hired longtime baseball professional Cedric Tallis as general manager, then gave him resources with which to work and a free hand to make decisions, in striking contrast to the approach taken by Finley in Kansas City. When the Royals played their first home game in April 1969, few mourned the departure of the Athletics, and no one regretted the departure of Charlie O. Finley. His antics continued in Oakland, only his team got much better. The bad news A's won three consecutive world championships between 1972 and 1974, and every single day Finley made life interesting with his shenanigans.

During the swinging sixties, the Cardinals recaptured the type of excellence they had enjoyed in the 1940s. Meanwhile, major-league baseball expanded twice; one of the beneficiaries of the latter expansion was Kansas City. The Athletics left Kansas City for Oakland, where they remain as of 2001. At no time, however, did Finley enjoy much return on his investment, as fans stayed away from even his good teams. Could it be that Finley himself drove them away with his pettiness and hijinks? In contrast to the Athletics, the Royals built a popular team and by the mid-1970s, much earlier than most expansion teams, began to put exceptionally competitive teams on the field. By the late 1970s the Royals had become the class of the American League's West Division. All the while the Cardinals seemed to decline and then to rebound in several exciting pennant races. Major-league baseball in Missouri was on the verge of a golden era as each of its two teams vied for championships. In 1985 they would meet in a climactic I-70 Interstate series that will long be remembered in the nation's heartland.

Building a Winner from Scratch in Kansas City

When the Kansas City Athletics departed for Oakland at the end of the 1967 season, some Missourians believed that major-league baseball had abandoned the western part of the state. Instead, Kansas City received an expansion team, the Royals, which began play in 1969. By the mid-1970s the Royals were winners. One of the most successful of all expansion clubs, the team finished either first or second in the American League West division twelve times in its first seventeen years. Its won-lost record of 860–701, .551, was the best in the division and the fourth best in the majors for the period 1969–1985. Beginning in 1976, the team took three successive division titles, but lost each year in the playoffs to the New York Yankees. In 1980 the Royals finally went to the World Series, but lost to the Philadelphia Phillies. Despite their postseason failures, the Royals were the best baseball team in Missouri in the 1970s. This chapter discusses the team's birth and its rise to dominance in the American League West.

The Birth of the Royals

During their thirteen-year sojourn in Kansas City, the Athletics never posted a winning record, and usually placed last or next to last in the American League. It took a true masochist to be a fan of the team, but the city did support the Athletics relatively well until the last season in 1967. That same support carried over to the expansion Royals, especially when it soon became apparent that the Royals were to be run in a manner bearing little resemblance to Charlie O. Finley's approach. In the Royals, Kansas City baseball fans found an organization

Ewing and Murial Kauffman, owners of the Kansas City Royals. Courtesy of the Kansas City Royals Baseball Club.

committed to building a winner and honest about how it planned to accomplish its goal.

This positive approach started at the top, with owner Ewing Kauffman. Kauffman entered major-league baseball through the most roundabout manner. He happened to attend a Chamber of Commerce luncheon in Kansas City in 1967 when Gabe Paul, president and general manager of the Cleveland Indians, spoke to the group about the need to mount a financial effort to bring to reality the expansion franchise promised by the American League. "I raised my hand and said I would be willing to put in a million dollars," Kauffman recalled, "not really doing it from anything but a civic standpoint." He was interested in sports—he owned a horse-racing stable—but unlike Charlie Finley, a baseball aficionado who had wanted to own a team since he made his first million, Kauffman was not a real fan, and certainly it was not his longtime ambition to own a baseball team. Even so, when no one else came forward with cash to create the franchise, he wound up as the sole owner.

With only a few weeks remaining before the next owners' meeting, Ernie Mehl and Earl Smith, a strong baseball supporter in Kansas City and owner of Smith-Grieves Printing Company, met with Kauffman at his office. They told him that no one else had stepped forward to join a consortium to purchase the new franchise, and that something had to be done or the American League would award the team to another city. "We need to show the American League there is somebody in Kansas City that is somewhat interested in baseball and financially can afford it," Mehl told Kauffman. Kauffman agreed, and promised to show the American League owners that he had the wherewithal to finance the team. Kauffman recalled, "Commerce Trust gave me a letter of credit for four million dollars, which they took with them to show that I could financially own a team." He obtained a letter of credit for another six million dollars to demonstrate an operating reserve should he become sole owner.

Kauffman's support proved fortunate for the future of Kansas City baseball. He had made a fortune in the pharmaceutical industry. His Marion Laboratories had consistently demonstrated its place as one of the most successful enterprises of its type in the United States, expanding broadly from its base in Kansas City into international markets. A driven overachiever, Kauffman had arrived at a time in his life when he was surveying the landscape for new challenges. Perhaps this entirely different enterprise of baseball would serve as a useful diversion. Certainly his wife, Muriel, hoped so. When he spoke with her, she told him to grab this new opportunity. As Kauffman recalled, "She said she thought I should do it because maybe I wouldn't work so hard at Marion. She thought baseball would give me a secondary interest and enjoyment and that possibly I might live longer."

Although four other ownership groups soon emerged in Kansas City to vie for the new team, Kauffman's bid seemed assured once he met with the major-league owners in November 1967 and told them how he planned to run the team. "If I get the ball team," he said, "I'll do what I did with the stable—hire professionals and turn the operation over to them. I'll lay down the financial policy. The baseball end, I'll leave to the baseball men." Pleased by this stark contrast to Charlie Finley, every owner in the American League—including Finley himself—voted to accept Kauffman as the owner of the new franchise in Kansas City. Indeed, he had the money, the experience, and the business and personal connections to make the team a success.

American League President Joe Cronin announced the final decision on January 11, 1968. "Mr. Kauffman was chosen," he said, "because of his fine business background, his connections in the public relations field, and his unending desire to own a major league franchise." Kauffman then made some remarks that were strikingly important to Kansas City baseball fans: "In my lifetime, this team will never be moved. If there is a financial loss, I can stand it. But I hope we can develop a successful organization." Unlike Finley, who made similar promises, Kauffman meant what he said. He had a strong philanthropic sense and a genuine desire to leave the world a better place than he found it. Years later he would try to give the team to the city, hoping it would become a public corporation much like the Green Bay Packers in the National Football League, but the American League owners blocked that action. After his death, his estate eventually sold the team to private investors.

Kauffman paid $5.3 million for the new Kansas City franchise, with on-field operations set to begin in 1969. Kansas City's new team, along with the expansion Seattle Pilots—a team that failed after one season and the next year became the Milwaukee Brewers—raised the number of American League teams to twelve. In 1969 the league was also split into two divisions, East and West. At the conclusion of the season, thereafter, the two division winners would meet in a best-of-five-game—later expanded to best-of-seven—League Championship Series to determine the American League's representative in the World Series.

American League Divisions in 1969

East Division	*West Division*
Baltimore Orioles	California Angels
Boston Red Sox	Chicago White Sox
Cleveland Indians	Kansas City Royals
Detroit Tigers	Minnesota Twins
New York Yankees	Oakland A's
Washington Senators	Seattle Pilots

Ewing Kauffman wasted no time in putting together a front-office staff to create his new team. He hired away from the California Angels baseball veteran Cedric Tallis as executive vice president and general manager, then left Tallis alone to establish operations. Tallis worked quickly to hire other officials for the front office, coaches, and scouts. He also established a nascent minor-league system and set researchers to work preparing for an expansion draft of mostly marginal players left unprotected by the established teams that would initially stock the Royals' roster.

Kauffman was a master salesman, and he quickly turned his attention to promoting the team in Kansas City. He held a competition to choose a name for the new team. More than seventeen thousand entries flooded into the franchise's makeshift offices in the Continental Hotel. The entries ran the gamut from various Indian tribes—Pawnees, Osages, and Kansa—to numerous animals—Bengals, Badgers, and Salukis—but none of those seemed quite right. Some suggestions tried variations of Kauffman's name—Kauffs, Kauffies, and Kaws-monats—but everyone agreed that those names were just plain silly. In the end Kauffman went with "Royals," which honored Kansas City's parade and pageant for the billion-dollar livestock industry known widely as the "American Royal." Kauffman personally chose blue and white—his horse-racing colors—for the team's colors, and had a logo designed that featured a gold crown.

Kauffman moved quickly to obtain sponsors, radio and television contracts, and support organizations. By February 1968 he had signed the Schlitz Brewing Company to sponsor television broadcasts for a minimum of sixteen road and twelve home games in 1969. He also organized the Royals Lancers, a community booster group to help sell season tickets. Membership was limited to individuals who sold at least seventy-five season tickets for the opening season; thirty-six professionals in the city qualified by the fall of 1968. Membership in the Royals Lancers quickly became another demarcation separating the elite from the ordi-nary in Kansas City. Members received admission to any American League game and jet fare to the Royals' spring training headquarters at Fort Myers, Florida. Royals board member Earl Smith quipped at one of the Lancers' meetings, "There's no reason in the world why we can't make this Lancer Club an expensive thing for Ewing Kauffman," and urged more effort by all to sign up season ticket holders. The Lancers proved a remarkably successful sales approach, and the Royals opened the 1969 season with a record 6,441 season ticket holders.

Meantime, Cedric Tallis brought aboard baseball veterans Charley Metro from the Chicago Cubs as director of personnel, Lou Gorman from the Bal-timore Orioles to serve as director of player development, and Joe Gordon to lead the team on the field. Tallis, Metro, Gorman, and Gordon agreed that they would emphasize signing young players and teaching them the game rather than trying to trade for experienced players. "We won't take players just because they have names," Tallis announced. "We have to build with young players; we're going for prospects." While they did not plan to finish last in 1969, everyone recognized that the team would not be a contender in its first season. It was hoped, however, that within five years the Royals would be ready to compete for the American League West Division title.

To support the youth movement, Kauffman sprang an additional four hun-dred thousand dollars to create a minor-league system. The Royals took a decid-edly unusual approach to this, founding the innovative Royals Baseball Acad-emy, which combined a junior college education for all signed players with intense instruction in the fine points of baseball. The academy was, according to Kauffman, "the only additional thing I could think of to build a winning team." Accordingly, the Royals expended more money on minor-league opera-tions than any other team in the majors. They had more scouts, coaches, and instructors than anyone else. "I wanted to bring Kansas City a winner in the quickest way possible," recalled Kauffman. "It soon became apparent to me that there were only four ways in which we could get better players, and not one of them was going to do us much good." Those four ways included the free agent draft, the minor-league draft, trades with other major-league teams, and buying players from other teams. The two drafts, in which no one team had an advantage over the others, were not likely to significantly help the Royals. "To trade well you have to be either lucky or have a lot of players other teams want," he recalled. "And money doesn't do that much for you." After all, Kauffman understood, every other owner was a millionaire as well. "The only thing I could do was to go outside the normal baseball avenues open to us and try to find better players. So I came up with the idea that you didn't have to play baseball all your life to be a good baseball player. That's what the old-timers in baseball thought. I thought that if you had the physical attributes necessary to be a baseball star, you could be taught baseball."

The Royals Baseball Academy opened its doors in Sarasota, Florida, in August 1970. Kauffman hired physicians and scientists to establish the attributes necessary for baseball stardom and to design tests that would measure those abilities in prospective players. This group, led by a young research psychologist who had worked both for NASA and the Naval Research Laboratory, Dr. Raymond Reilly, homed in on four physical abilities necessary for success in baseball: speed of foot, excellent eyesight, quick reflexes and overall agility, and outstanding body balance. If those attributes, which everyone agreed could not be taught, were present, then the athlete could learn the specific skills required to excel at baseball. The team also came up with a battery of personality tests to assess the character of potential baseball players. The Royals set about looking for young athletes "with a strong need to achieve something of significance . . . who are well above average in intelligence . . . and have a good memory for facts and figures."

The first thirty-five players in the academy were selected using the criteria and tests developed by Reilly's team. These athletes had been picked from among those trying out in forty-one separate states. They did not identify themselves principally as baseball players, but all were outstanding athletes in a variety of sports. For the next two years they spent their mornings at Manatee Junior College and their afternoons working on baseball skills. They received two years' worth of tuition, room, and board, plus a sliding-scale stipend that started at one hundred dollars per month and went up the longer they were in the program. Several of the academy graduates eventually made it to the major leagues and one, Frank White, went on to star with the Royals for eighteen seasons between 1973 and 1990. But the academy proved too expensive—it cost more than six hundred thousand dollars per year—and closed its doors in 1974. Its physical and psychological tests, however, soon became a standard means of measuring the potential of all baseball players, and with some modifications and increased sophistication are still used.

"Trader" Tallis and the Rise of the Royals

The players who took the field for the Royals in their first game on April 8, 1969, had virtually no experience in major-league play. But the 1969 Royals exhibited some signs of promise. Lou Piniella, a twenty-six-year-old rookie acquired during spring training from the Seattle Pilots for outfielder Steve Whitaker and pitcher John Gelnar, represented a steal of the first order by Tallis, who had learned that the Pilots thought Piniella did not fit in and wanted to unload him. Allowed to play every day in Kansas City, Piniella proceeded to bat .282 and win Rookie of the Year honors. Piniella would go on to play five productive seasons for the Royals before moving on to the New York Yankees for eleven more seasons and then becoming one of the game's best managers in the 1990s.

That first year the Royals finished the season 69–93, twenty-eight games behind the division-winning Minnesota Twins, not too good but still better than either the White Sox or the Pilots. The 1970 season was even worse, as the team finished with a 65–97 record. There were two bright spots, however, as Tallis's efforts to obtain quality players bore additional fruit.

With lead-footed but powerful Piniella in right field, the Royals added on December 1, 1969, one of the most important players ever to wear Royals blue, Amos Otis. "AO," as everyone in Kansas City called him, was another of Cedric Tallis's steals. Never viewed as a real prospect by the New York Mets, they let him and pitcher Bob Johnson go in exchange for Joe Foy. Johnson helped the Royals in 1970 with an 8–13 record, the best among all Royals pitchers, but it was Otis who became a mainstay. In 1970 he batted .284, and led the American League with 36 doubles and 33 stolen bases. The thin, handsome, dignified African American also played a superb center field; he would win three Gold Glove awards over the course of his career. Otis's glove work provided the Royals with a critical component on all championship clubs: strong defense up the middle. On many a summer night the thousands who turned out to watch the Royals' home stands would cheer Otis's excellent defensive plays and his stance at the plate as he stared down opposing pitchers. Periodically one could hear cowbells ringing and the trademark loud, low, long "AaaaaaaOoooooo" from fans. It would be hard to overestimate the importance of AO as a catalyst for the Royals. His presence on the field served as a model for his teammates, and his

The Royals' first star, "AO," Amos Otis. Courtesy of the Kansas City Royals Baseball Club.

popularity with the crowds in Kansas City ensured that a large audience turned out to watch the games.

Another important acquisition took place on June 13, 1970, when Cookie Rojas came over from the Cardinals to play second base. Rojas had eight years of major-league experience with the Cubs, Phillies, and Cardinals. With the Royals he immediately established himself as an All-Star who averaged .260–.270 at the plate while providing a good glove in the infield. Tallis had earlier acquired shortstop Fred Patek and two minor-leaguers from the Pirates for Bob Johnson and two other minor-leaguers on December 2, 1970. "Little Freddie," who supposedly stood 5'5" but probably was shorter, proved to be another happy acquisition for the Royals. Another of the great glove/poor bat shortstops that every major-league team seemed to have at the time, Patek played for the Royals through the 1970s. Rojas, Otis, and Patek anchored the team's strong defense up the middle.

Two additional key players came to the Royals via trades during the early 1970s. On December 2, 1971, first baseman John Mayberry came over from the Astros for two players. The power-hitting first baseman never got much opportunity to play in Houston, but he responded as a regular in Kansas City. While in Royals blue, Mayberry's bat terrorized American League pitchers for the next six years. The Royals also acquired outfielder/designated hitter Hal McRae and pitcher Wayne Simpson from the Reds on November 30, 1972. Simpson, by then a washed-up starting pitcher, never helped the Royals much, but McRae spent the next fifteen years in a Royals uniform. In the process the thoughtful African American player compiled a lifetime batting average of .290 and became a reliable RBI man, leading the league in 1982 with 133 runs batted in.

The string of deals to bring Piniella, Otis, Rojas, Patek, Mayberry, and McRae to Kansas City rank as some of the best snookering ever done by one general manager to his colleagues. Cedric Tallis looks like a genius in hindsight, but many people criticized his trades at the time. They seemed to believe what most of the baseball world accepted about these players, that Piniella and others would never become major-leaguers. Instead, the Royals, with a lineup including six everyday starters who were castoffs from other clubs, moved in three years from also-ran expansion team to perennial contender in the American League West. Tallis had been lucky, no question about it, but it was luck born of hard work and strict attention to building the team on youth. With the exception of Rojas, none of the Royals had gotten much of an opportunity to play with their previous teams. They had been written off before they had a chance.

With the help of excellent trades, the Royals contended for the division title in 1971, their third year in the league. Ironically, they finished behind the newly invincible Oakland A's. The Royals were a distant second, sixteen games behind the A's, but they were competitive and Kauffman was delighted. The Royals needed to add more good players before they would be in position to make serious runs at division titles, however. They certainly needed pitchers. Paul Splittorff was the first pitcher of note to come to the Royals. A product of the team's farm system, Splittorff was the first player originally signed by the Royals to make it to the majors, and in 1973 he became the team's first twenty-game winner. A control pitcher with a fine sinkerball, Splittorff would prove enormously important to the Royals' winning teams of the 1970s and early 1980s. Upon his retirement in 1984, he was the club's all-time leader in games and innings pitched, starts, wins, and losses.

There were other pitchers who were nearly as significant. Steve Busby hurled no-hitters in each of his first two full major-league seasons, 1973 and 1974. He won sixteen games for the Royals in 1973 and was named American League Rookie Pitcher of the Year. During his next two seasons Busby set a Royals record

Hal McRae. Courtesy of the Kansas City Royals Baseball Club.

with a 22–14 tally in 1974 and then went 18–12 in 1975. After three stellar seasons, however, knee and rotator cuff injuries took their toll, and in 1980 he retired after the Royals' first trip to the World Series. Another pitcher, Larry Gura, also blossomed with the Royals, going 88–49 from 1976 through 1982. A crafty starter, he was the Royals' Pitcher of the Year in 1978, when he went 16–4 with a 2.72 earned run average, and won eighteen games in both 1980 and 1982. The fine-fielding Gura also went through both 1980 and 1981 without an error.

Two other pitchers came into their own in the late 1970s for the Royals. Dennis Leonard joined the team in 1974 and posted an unimpressive 0–4 record. But in 1975 he went 15–7, and the redhead became the Royals' Pitcher of the Year in 1975, 1977, and 1979. He employed a hard fastball, curve, and slider to average eighteen wins a year between 1975 and 1980, including twenty-win seasons in 1977, 1978, and 1980. In the bullpen, Dan Quisenberry employed striking control and a submarine delivery to keep hitters off-stride. His bread-and-butter pitch was a sharp-breaking slider. Only three times in ten years did he issue more than fifteen walks in a season despite pitching more than 125 innings five times. In his first full season in 1979, Quisenberry won a dozen games and saved thirty-three while appearing seventy-five times. He led the American League in saves five times, including a record-setting forty-five in 1983 and again the following season. Five times he received American League Fireman of the Year honors. Quisenberry played ten of his twelve major-league seasons with the Royals and retired in 1990.

The final pieces of the puzzle came from the Royals' farm system. Frank White, a graduate of the Royals Baseball Academy, joined the big-league team in 1973. White played behind Cookie Rojas for several years but then took over the regular duties at second base in 1976, just in time to play on a succession of division- and pennant-winning teams. In 1977 White played sixty-two consecutive games without an error. He collected eight Gold Glove awards in his career and is the only second baseman in American League history to win six straight fielding awards. Three times he led the league's second basemen in fielding percentage, and in 1988 he made only four errors in 150 games. By the time of his retirement in 1990, White had been a Royal for eighteen seasons, longer than anyone else in the franchise's history, except for a teammate who also made the club in 1973, Hall of Famer George Brett.

George Brett: The King of the Royals and His Court

George Brett was the most important player ever to join the Royals, and if no one else had ever come out of the team's farm system, he alone would have been worth the price. Brett owned third base for fifteen years in Kansas City. Later in his career he moved to first base when he was no longer quick enough to play third. Never quite the iron man that Stan Musial had been on the diamond, Brett nevertheless played most of the time, and his commitment to the working-class ideals of showing up and doing the best one could always showed on the field. No one ever complained that Brett was an overpaid celebrity who did not try his best in every game, something that was said of many of baseball's other superstars.

Submariner relief pitcher Dan Quisenberry. Courtesy of the Kansas
City Royals Baseball Club.

Brett's loyalty to the Royals was legendary. Through a twenty-year career he
remained a Royal, despite opportunities that came repeatedly when free agency
made it the norm for baseball players to go anywhere for a higher salary. Brett
came to love Kansas City and decided of his own accord that he would make it
his home. Although a surfer from southern California, Brett, like Stan Musial in

St. Louis, embraced his adopted city. Also like Musial, Brett conducted himself with honor and dignity both on the ball field and off.

One of the hardest-working players in the majors, Brett became a perennial All-Star and the team leader in almost all offensive categories. He was the only major-league player to win batting titles in three different decades, leading the American League in hitting in 1976, 1980, and 1990. He earned the Gold Glove award in 1985 as the league's top defensive third baseman. He was the only player in history to have more than 3,000 hits, 300 home runs, 600 doubles, 100 triples, and 200 stolen bases. He joined the elite company of Musial, Henry Aaron, Willie Mays, Carl Yastrzemski, Al Kaline, and Dave Winfield as the only players with 3,000 hits and 300 home runs. His career statistics of a .305 batting average, 3,154 hits, 317 home runs, and 1,586 RBIs assured him a place in Cooperstown, and he, like Stan Musial, was elected on the first ballot to the Hall of Fame.

For all that Brett's accomplishments on the field meant to the Royals, there was something more that he symbolized for the team and for the fans in Kansas City and the rest of the Midwest. The Midwest is more traditional—not necessarily more conservative—than many parts of the United States. Its residents have long believed intensely in the importance of hard work, fair play, honorable

The greatest Royal of them all, George Brett. Courtesy of the Kansas City Royals Baseball Club.

dealings, and loyalty to ideals that call forth humankind to make the world a better place. George Brett, number 5 in a powder-blue Royals uniform, personified all of those attributes more than anyone else ever identified with Kansas City.

In their book *Major League Stadiums,* authors Dan Dickinson and Kieran Dickinson astutely observed the people who went to Kansas City Royals games. "More than in most places," they noted, "being a Royals fan is an expression of solidarity not just with a team, but with a community and, indeed, with a way of life." The conduct of players off the field is just as important as their conduct during games. The authors learned from one of the fans at a Royals game that even if Oakland A's slugger Jose Canseco wanted to come to Kansas City, he "wouldn't make it here. He's too fast-track. We like our people wholesome." Brett, although he had faults, proved the perfect Royals player for these denizens of the Midwest. Fans universally praised Brett as the best that baseball had to offer. The Dickinsons pressed one woman at a Royals game for an answer to what she liked best about Brett: His home runs? His batting average? Possibly his single status? "Well," she declared, "he's never embarrassed us." It is a telling commentary on both Kansas City and its greatest baseball player. The Dickinsons concluded with an insightful comment: "This is an audience that, in an age of rampant 'me first' individualism, sees the connectedness between people, that in a time in which values are 'relative,' feels, however unfashionably, that there are some standards worth holding to. There's a place for such fans." Brett fit perfectly into this society.

Joe Posnanski, a columnist for the *Kansas City Star,* tried to explain the significance of Brett's life and career for Kansas City at the time of his induction into the National Baseball Hall of Fame in 1999. Posnanski's comments are also telling:

> George Brett touches the heart of his town. Len Dawson [of the Kansas City Chiefs] was cheered and booed and cheered louder still. Satchel Paige was a walking, talking legend from the day he walked into town. [Golfer] Tom Watson has carried this city in his golf bag around the world. Otis Taylor [of the Chiefs] caught everything thrown to him. Maurice Greene can fly. Buck O'Neil speaks truths in a beautiful voice that's always just a skip away from singing. But, even so, it's Brett that scratches the nerves, makes people happy, makes people angry, makes people cry, like no athlete who has wandered through this city. So, they ask, what George Brett means to Kansas City. "He means better times," I tell them. "And he means baseball."

Just like Stan Musial across the state, Brett remained in his city after retirement and wields considerable influence long after his departure from the playing field.

Contention

In the Royals' fifth season, 1973, the team moved into Royals Stadium, a baseball-only facility that is part of the Harry S. Truman Sports Complex about seven miles east of Kansas City on I-70. On April 10, 1973, the Royals played their first game there, treating the 39,464 fans in attendance to a 12–1 romp over the Texas Rangers. The beautiful new ballpark altered the trend toward multipurpose facilities such as Busch Memorial Stadium in St. Louis. Expansive, open-air Royals Stadium had an Astroturf playing field and sliding pits at each base and around home plate. That made it a hot place to play day games in the summer, and it was tough on the knees. Only in the 1990s did the Royals go to a more traditional grass surface. Two features have dominated their ballpark. The first is the water spectacular, the largest privately funded fountain in the world, extending behind the outfield wall from the right-field to left-field bullpens and shaped in the form of the number one. The second feature is a twelve-story-high scoreboard shaped like the Royals emblem and containing 16,320 lightbulbs, most of them on the forty-by-sixty-foot screen. Appropriately, on July 24, 1973, Royals Stadium hosted the fortieth All-Star Game. In that game Cincinnati's Johnny Bench blasted a mammoth homer to spark a 7–1 National League win. Even so, the Royals' John Mayberry and Amos Otis combined for three of the five American League hits.

In 1973 the Royals made their first serious run for the division title. A mid-summer spurt carried them into first place in August, but from there they leveled off to another second-place finish, six games behind the Oakland A's. The Royals finished in second place for a third time in 1975, when Oakland won the division again. This time it looked like the team was on the verge of greatness. They went 91–71, the best record they had posted. It had been a frustrating experience for Ewing Kauffman, the Royals, and the fans of Kansas City to play second fiddle to Charlie Finley's A's during the early 1970s. The Athletics had become every bit as good in Oakland as they had been bad in Kansas City, winning World Series championships in 1972, 1973, and 1974. It was a dynasty as great as any the legendary Philadelphia Athletics had boasted under Connie Mack. But 1975 was the last year of A's dominance. Finley was strapped for cash and had been caught in an underhanded breach of contract, which freed Catfish Hunter to pursue offers from other clubs. Hunter soon signed with the Yankees. Finley then proceeded to trade and sell other players, and beginning in 1977 the Athletics dropped to the bottom of the division. Diehard Kansas City fans could not have been more pleased, for with the demise of the A's, the Royals became the class of the American League West.

Royals Stadium, taken at the time of the All-Star game held there in 1973. Courtesy of Special Collections, Kansas City Public Library.

Division Titles, but No Respect

The frustration of almost winning the 1975 West Division race proved too much for Ewing Kauffman. In a fit of exasperation unusual for him, he fired manager Jack McKeon and replaced him with Whitey Herzog. Herzog was a midwesterner from New Athens, Illinois, who grew up living and dying by the fortunes of the St. Louis Cardinals. A ballplayer of no particular distinction, the White Rat—an appellation Herzog liked—studied the game like few others and developed keen understanding of its finer points. He demanded a style of play in Kansas City called "Whiteyball" that emphasized good pitching, outstanding foot speed, and great defense. In typical journalist hyperbole, the news media labeled Herzog a "genius" for bringing this style of play to Kansas City, as if he had invented that type of baseball. But generations of Cardinals had played that same type of ball, as those surviving were quick to point out in the mid-1970s. Herzog preached getting on base any way possible—a walk is as good as a hit—then starting the runner, slapping the ball on the ground, and winning the game during the ensuing confusion. Herzog thought a stolen base was even better than a home run; it created excitement in the ballpark and frustration for the opposition. All of Herzog's teams were fast, and most of the players were aggressive base runners. One wit opined that Whitey should coach track and field rather than baseball.

Under Herzog the Royals won three successive division crowns in 1976, 1977, and 1978. All the while they played "Whiteyball" with the best of them. In 1976 the Royals took the division lead two months into the season and held it to the end, winning 90 and losing 72. One of the most interesting dramas of the regular season involved the race between third baseman George Brett and designated hitter Hal McRae for the American League batting championship. Officially, Brett won the title with a .333 average and McRae was a close second at .332. But who actually deserved the batting title has been a source of debate. Many who saw the last game, and some who were part of it, still don't know what happened. Some said it was fixed. Some said there were racial implications. "To this day, I don't think anybody knows the truth," Dean Vogelaar, then the Royals public relations director, said in 1999.

The batting title came down to not only the last game but also the last inning of the season. And all of the contenders were on the same field. With the Minnesota Twins in Kansas City for a season-ending, three-game series, it was clear that someone in Royals Stadium would emerge with a batting title. Kansas City's McRae and Brett and Minnesota's Rod Carew and Lyman Bostock were one-two-three-four in the batting race. Bostock fell out of the running when he hurt his thumb in the series opener and missed the last two games; he finished the season batting .323. Carew, who remained in the race until midway through the last game, finished at .331.

Going into the finale, McRae led Brett by .00005. The Royals had already clinched their first division title, so the pressure to win was off. Under normal circumstances Herzog probably would have given his regulars an off day to prepare for the League Championship Series. But Brett and McRae had to play to resolve the batting championship. Each player was two for three heading into the bottom of the ninth inning, when both were scheduled to bat again. Officially, McRae was at .33269, and Brett was at .33229. McRae of course needed only a hit to ice the title, while Brett somehow had to pass McRae. In his last at bat, Brett lofted a routine fly ball to the outfield, which Twins left fielder Steve Brye should have caught easily. Brye was playing unusually deep, however, and he broke in the wrong direction. The ball landed about ten feet in front of him and then bounced over his head to the left-field wall. Brett circled the bases for an inside-the-park home run and finished the day three for four. No one was more excited by this than McRae, who greeted Brett at home plate with a big smile and a high five. McRae knew that he could still take the batting crown, but it would require a clean hit. Unfortunately, he grounded out to the shortstop.

While happy for his teammate, McRae believed that the Twins had conspired to let Brett win the batting title. He believed that Minnesota's manager, Gene Mauch, had ordered Brye to misplay Brett's fly ball. He explicitly cited racism as the reason for Mauch's action, saying after the game, "This is America, and not that much has changed. Too bad in 1976 things are still like that." As he walked back to the dugout McRae doffed his batting helmet to a standing ovation by the Royals' faithful, then turned and displayed his middle finger to the Twins dugout. There must have been something to his assertion, for Mauch was incensed and charged on to the field. Both benches then emptied, and it took a few minutes for the umpires to restore order.

Brett said after the game that Brye's play surprised him. "I swear," Brett commented, "he just stopped and let it bounce in front of him." But Steve Brye has resolutely maintained that he misplayed the ball and did not let it drop intentionally. So has Mauch, who was clearly shaken by McRae's allegations. "This thing hurts me more than anything that has ever happened in my thirty-five years in baseball," Mauch said later. Perhaps Mauch did not rig the batting championship in 1976. I doubt that he did, and I very much doubt racism played a role in the episode. Mauch would have cheered had either Carew or Bostock, both of whom were black, taken the batting title. No one will ever know. The real problem for the Royals was whether or not the outcome of the batting race would fester and destroy the camaraderie between Brett and McRae as the team headed into the playoffs against the Yankees. Apparently, it did not have too many ramifications. The next day the other members of the Royals saw Brett and McRae in the dugout during practice talking and joking about the turn of events. McRae insists to the present that he still does not know if Mauch had Brye misplay the ball, but still believes that racism is present in American society. Regardless, he adds, the incident should not diminish the accomplishments of George Brett, who won three batting titles. "One of them was won over a teammate in circumstances that could have torn apart their relationship," recalled McRae, "but it didn't." For his part, Brett said, "Hal and I were great friends prior to that. I think, that day, he felt cheated. I think after that day, he was fine with it."

Both players carried their hot bats into the postseason, but the Yankees took the pennant in a heartbreaking five-game playoff series. The fifth and deciding game proved frustrating for the Royals. They scored first, getting two runs in the first inning on John Mayberry's home run. But the Yankees tied the game when they came to bat. Kansas City retook the lead in the second inning. New York went ahead again in the third and increased its lead to 6–3 in the sixth, but in the top of the eighth, George Brett's three-run homer tied the score once again. The stage was set for Yankee third baseman Chris Chambliss, who won the team's thirtieth American League pennant with his first-pitch home run in the bottom of the ninth inning. It was a gut-wrenching experience to watch Freddie Patek bent over, in tears and clutching his face, at his shortstop position, while Chambliss rounded the bases to seal the victory. Royals fans took some joy in watching the Cincinnati Reds crush the Yankees in the World Series four games to none.

For two more years the Royals dominated the American League West but failed to stop the Yankees in the League Championship Series. In 1977 they again entered the playoffs with high expectations. While they had not moved into the division lead until mid-August, they were nearly unstoppable the rest of the way and finished the season with a record of 102–60, still the best the team has ever done. The Royals boasted a pitching staff that led the league in earned run average and a balanced offense that included four players each with more than twenty home runs and eighty RBIs. One of them was Al Cowens, a journeyman outfielder who had come to the club from the farm system in 1974 and had a wonderful season in 1977. He batted .312, homered 23 times, and drove in 112 runs. The playoff opponent was again the Yankees. This time Kansas City won the first game, and the teams traded victories through the first four games. In Game Five Kansas City took a lead into the ninth inning. Everyone started to celebrate, as it looked as though the Royals were about to take the pennant. But with the pennant in sight, the Royals gave up three runs in the top of the ninth, then failed to score themselves in the bottom of the inning as ace reliever Sparky Lyle held them off to give the Yankees the pennant. This time, New York went on to win the World Series from the Los Angeles Dodgers.

Changes came to the Royals in the aftermath of the disappointing postseason. Herzog was mad at first baseman John Mayberry because of his apparent lack of hustle and sent him packing to the Toronto Blue Jays. Mayberry had slumped to .232 with 13 home runs in 1976, but did drive in 95 runs as the Royals won their first division title. The slump continued in 1977 as he hit .230, although he did have 23 home runs. He also made himself unpopular in Kansas City by sitting out the last game of the playoffs with a toothache (he had homered in Game One). Herzog took the opportunity to deal the man who stood as the club's career leader in home runs and RBIs. Second baseman Cookie Rojas also retired at the end of the 1977 season. He had been a spot starter for two seasons, with Frank White filling in well at second base. In 1978 prospect Willie Wilson would begin playing every day; he had come up from the farm for brief stints

The fleet-footed Willie Wilson. Courtesy of the Kansas City Royals
Baseball Club.

with the Royals in both 1976 and 1977. Once Wilson started playing every day,
he would hit .300 for four successive seasons, and by 1988 he had stolen more
than thirty bases in eleven consecutive seasons. In 1980 Wilson became only the
second player to collect one hundred hits from each side of the plate in a season.

In 1978 Whitey Herzog had his team humming again, and although the division race was a bit tighter than the previous year the Royals finished with a 92–70 record, five games ahead of the Texas Rangers and the California Angels. In the playoffs the Royals again met the Yankees, but this time the result was not as close. The Royals tied the series with a big win in Game Two, but the Yankees came back to take the next two games by one run each for their third straight flag. Once again New York defeated the Dodgers in the World Series.

The First Pennant: 1980

The next year, 1979, the Royals slumped to second place in the American League West, finishing 88–77, three games behind the division-winning California Angels. The Royals' poor showing in 1979 was too much for Ewing Kauffman. He fired Whitey Herzog and brought in Jim Frey to manage the team. Kauffman believed that Herzog had taken the Royals as far as he could. Someone else would have to lead them to the next level. Frey led the Royals to the American League pennant in 1980, his first year as a major-league manager. Interestingly, he would be fired before the end of the 1981 season. It seems that while his abilities as a judge of talent and as a leader were beyond reproach, he certainly failed in making tactical decisions. The 1980 World Series demonstrated that fact.

Frey's Royals came out of the gate fast in 1980 to overwhelm the rest of the division. Despite a month-long decline in September, Kansas City finished with a record of 97–65, fourteen games ahead of second-place Oakland. The most interesting drama on the field in the regular season was George Brett's exploits with his bat.

Throughout the year, Brett chased one of the Holy Grails of baseball, a single-season batting average of .400. Boston Red Sox slugger Ted Williams had been the last player to attain the goal, batting .406 in 1941. Brett had a shot in 1980. On July 10 his average stood at .341, certainly an excellent mark but not one to make anyone swoon. But then something happened. He started pasting the ball all over the park, and out of it as well, as he hammered twenty-four home runs for the season. By July 18 his average had risen to .377. By the end of the month he was hitting .386 and people were starting to take notice. *Kansas City Star* sportswriter Joe McGuff dared to ask Brett about the likelihood of hitting .400. "Don't ask me that," Brett said. "I don't know how long this hot streak is going to last."

Meantime, Brett continued to stroke the ball better than at any time in his career, and his average finally reached .401 on August 17, when he went four-for-four with two doubles and five RBIs. Conservative talk show host Rush Limbaugh recalled:

I was working in the Royals' marketing department. . . . When he hit that double, the one that put him over .400, and he stood on second base and raised his hands, (30,000) people stood. There was a thunderous roar. After the game, I called him and said, "Do you have any idea what you mean to this community? Do you realize they are living their lives vicariously through you?" . . . That was the kind of stuff he didn't want to hear. He was very humble about it.

Throughout the rest of the season Brett's average hovered around .400, and the longer it did, the more media attention it drew. Soon journalists who could not name the starting lineup of the Royals a month before were traveling with the team. The pressure became acute and Brett admittedly felt it keenly. The pitchers worked him very carefully. They walked him constantly. In Cleveland, he got hurt swinging the bat and missed eleven games. When he came back, he continued to flirt with .400 but he could never quite get above it. Perhaps Brett did not see the ball like before; maybe he did not feel as free. Certainly reporters hounded him and fielders made great catches. Balls he had clobbered in August now seemed to be weak fly outs. He went 4 for 27 as the season drew to a close and his average dropped to .384. Brett then got 10 hits in his last 19 at-bats for the season and finished at .390—not the magic .400, but still the highest major-league batting average in thirty-nine years.

Other players on the Royals also had career years in 1980. Reliever Dan Quisenberry enjoyed his first big season (12 wins, 33 saves), and starter Dennis Leonard came back from an off-year to record his third twenty-win season in four years. Willie Wilson, who had taken over patrolling center field, had an outstanding year, batting .326 and leading the league in hits with 230 and runs scored with 133.

But most important, in 1980 the Royals finally beat the Yankees—in a three-game sweep—to win the League Championship Series and capture their first pennant. They looked forward to a World Series against the Philadelphia Phillies, historically one of the worst teams in the National League. The Phillies had played in only two World Series prior to 1980, in 1915 and in 1950, and had been swept both times. Could Kauffman and the Royals finally bring a World Series championship to Kansas City after so many near misses?

The fortunes of the Philadelphia Phillies had paralleled those of the Royals in the late 1970s. Like the Royals, the Phillies had become a powerhouse within their division, winning National League East titles in 1976, 1977, and 1978, but only to lose each year in the League Championship Series. After slipping in the 1979 campaign, the Phillies roared back in 1980 to take their division and the National League pennant. They were led by two future Hall of Fame players, left-handed pitcher Steve Carlton (whom the Cardinals let go in 1971) and third baseman Mike Schmidt, as well as by first baseman Pete Rose, who should be in the Hall of Fame because of his excellence on the field but who has thus far been barred from enshrinement because of a gambling scandal.

The 1980 World Series was the first to be played exclusively on artificial turf, and it made for fast and exciting games. There was not much subtlety to the play, however, as each team hammered the other's pitching staff for lots of runs and not a few homers. In the end, three come-from-behind victories allowed the Phillies to win the series four games to two and claim the first World Champion-ship in their ninety-seven-year history. Although the Royals almost matched Philadelphia in offense (.290 to .294 in average and 23 to 27 in runs), they struck out 49 times. Kansas City's lead-off hitter, Willie Wilson, set the all-time World Series mark with 12 whiffs. Philadelphia took Game One 7–6 and Game Two 6–4 at their home park, Veterans Stadium. Interestingly, and the media loved the titillating nature of the story, George Brett had to leave Game Two after the sixth inning because he was suffering from hemorrhoids. He jetted back to Kansas City early for hemorrhoid surgery prior to Game Three of the series. Brett later quipped that he had been a flaming asshole until he had surgery, and thereafter he was a perfect asshole. When asked to comment on the problem, he replied, "I think my problems are all behind me now." Back in Kansas City for Game Three, the Royals took the Phillies 4–3 in a ten-inning contest. The Royals also won Game Four, 5–3, to tie the series. But then the Phillies came back to win the next two games by scores of 4–3 and 4–1.

Manager Jim Frey deserved the principal blame for the World Series loss. In particular, he let the Phillies see too much of ace closer Dan Quisenberry. The submariner was always best when brought in late in a game after opposing bat-ters had seen a different type of pitcher. Quisenberry's unique delivery always forced hitters to adjust, and he was most effective when facing the order only once. While Frey often had misused Quisenberry in the season by bringing him on to relieve in the seventh inning, the strategy did not backfire until the World Series against the good-hitting Phillies, who hammered Quisenberry after they had acclimated to his pitching style. Pete Rose summarized it best when he told a reporter, "The guy [Frey] is giving us the World Series by letting us look at Quisenberry's delivery so much." Not surprisingly, Ewing Kauffman's support for Frey wavered the next season, and when the Royals failed to play up to ex-pectations, Frey was fired and replaced by well-liked coach Dick Howser.

For all their success in their first dozen years of existence, the Royals never quite made it as champions of the baseball world. The seemingly mechanical efficiency with which they raced through seasons and captured division flags belied what can only be understood as an underlying lack of spirit on the part of the team when it came to the postseason. Some observers commented that the Royals were antiseptic, as sterile and rhythmless as the beautiful Royals Stadium in which they played. Little in the way of personality or character showed through.

No one would ever favorably compare the Royals' teams of the 1970s to the brawling, feuding, rambunctious, and championship-winning Yankees and A's, their main competitors during this era. The A's, for instance, fought incessantly with each other and their owner over everything imaginable. They had personality and character and a strange attraction that commanded everyone's attention. Today even the most casual baseball aficionado knows the names of Catfish Hunter, Vida Blue, Reggie Jackson, Joe Rudi, Bert Campaneris, Gene Tenace, and others. Their faces and their exploits are indelibly etched in memory. Likewise, the memory of the "Bronx Zoo" Yankees, to use Sparky Lyle's parlance, still energizes baseball lovers long after they won their championships, mowing down the Royals and their National League challengers seemingly at will. Again, Catfish Hunter, Reggie Jackson, Thurman Munson, Chris Chambliss, Craig Nettles, Bucky Dent, Willie Randolph, Mickey Rivers, Rich Gossage, Ron Guidry, and the rest beckon the fans to root for them—or perhaps as likely, to root against them—across the divide of time.

The A's and the Yankees, whether one loved or hated them, provoked the passions of the fans. The Royals of the 1970s never evoked that type of response. One might counter by noting that the Royals played in a small-market city in which few fans beyond the borders were exposed to the team, its players, and its quest for excellence. Certainly, that is true. One might also respond by adding that the Royals inspired passions in the region, if not the nation, and that might be true as well. But there seems to have been something more. They were a consistent, almost mechanical team that churned out victories like General Motors churns out cars. Kauffman designed the team as such, without ever quite reaching the pinnacle of success, and for many years that was enough. When one looked deep down into the soul of the Royals for the inner strength out of which champions came, however, there was not much there.

The poster child for the Royals of this era may have been Amos Otis. AO was a superb athlete who consistently hit well, played excellent defense, ran fast, jumped high, and very nearly leaped tall buildings at a single bound. An honorable and justifiably proud man, he had a sculpted body that men aspired to and women coveted. One of my college girlfriends who was not a serious baseball fan said she always loved going to Royals games so she could watch him from behind as he strolled to the plate, wiggled his butt in the batter's box, and flitted around the bases. Otis had a wonderful seventeen-year career, mostly with the

Royals, and ranks as one of the greatest players in the team's history. Yet he never quite made it to the pinnacle. It is sad to say, but seemingly true for the Royals of this era, that they did not have the intangible qualities necessary to win the big games.

But the team developed character through the strife and adversity during their years near the summit. The players earned the soul necessary to achieve a championship in the early 1980s, when, despite being viewed as the most-talented team in the American League West, they suffered through four years of bitter frustration and soul searching. George Brett, as usual, led the way. In the early 1980s the Royals developed the mental toughness, the strength of character, and the talented arms, legs, and especially hearts necessary to win a World Series. When next they journeyed to the fall classic in 1985, they were a strikingly different team from the one that had been mangled by the Phillies in 1980. Although the Royals had many of the same players, they were not the same men they had been before. Older and wiser, they would show in 1985 that they had the inner strength of champions.

Showdown on I-70

While the Kansas City Royals developed into an outstanding baseball team by the mid-1970s, the once mighty St. Louis Cardinals declined precipitously after the pennant of 1968. For fourteen years the Cardinals remained mired in mediocrity. While they sometimes challenged other teams for the National League East championship, they usually were at or just below .500, somewhere in the middle of the pack. But finally, in 1982 the Cardinals won another World Series, and in 1985 and 1987 the team took National League pennants but not the world championship. The result was that during the 1980s, Missouri, with superior teams in the Royals and Cardinals, figured prominently in major-league baseball, especially in 1985, when the two teams met in a climactic cross-state World Series.

Into the Wilderness

In the 1960s the Cardinals, along with the Los Angeles Dodgers, dominated the National League. The Cardinals and Dodgers each took three pennants and two World Series titles, while no other team in the league won more than one pennant. But beginning in 1969, the Cardinals began a journey into the wilderness that was just as trying as that of the children of Israel, even if it was only one-quarter as long. With the expansion of the National League to twelve teams in 1969, the owners agreed to align into two divisions:

East Division	*West Division*
Chicago Cubs	Atlanta Braves
Montreal Expos	Cincinnati Reds
New York Mets	Houston Astros
Philadelphia Phillies	Los Angeles Dodgers
Pittsburgh Pirates	San Diego Padres
St. Louis Cardinals	San Francisco Giants

This divisional lineup made little rational sense from a geographical perspective. What could possibly motivate the owners to place the Braves and the Reds in the National League West, while the Cardinals and the Cubs played in the East? In reality, geography did not motivate the owners in the slightest. Team rivalries and competitive balance had more to do with the new alignment than anything else. In this lineup, moreover, the Cardinals looked to be the East's dominant team. Of the other teams in the division, only the Pirates had won a pennant in the previous decade (in 1960). The Cubs and Phillies were generally pathetic, having failed to take a pennant since 1945 and 1950 respectively. The Mets, an expansion team in 1962, had never had a winning season, and the Expos were one of the two new teams joining the National League in 1969. In contrast, the West had the Reds, Dodgers, and Giants, who always played strong baseball and fought it out for pennants. In this situation, the Cardinals were expected to win at least the East division every year.

The Cardinals certainly disappointed all their fans. For the next fourteen years they failed to take any championships. Instead the Pirates and Phillies, both of whom had been rebuilding throughout the 1960s, emerged to win ten of the first twelve division titles from 1969 to 1980. In only two seasons did the Cardinals even threaten this hegemony. In 1973 and 1974 the team ran neck-and-neck with the eventual division champions, but finished one and one-half games behind at the end of each season. The Cardinals were not really a bad team, but they finished the years 1969–1981 with 1,020 wins and 1,018 losses, for a .50076 record. At least they did well at the gate, averaging 1,491,376 people per season in home attendance.

In the early 1970s the Cardinals' greatest players of the era, Bob Gibson and Lou Brock, continued to play exceptionally well. Gibson retired after the 1975 season with a string of team records, including most wins in Cardinals history. He became only the second pitcher in major-league history to fan three thousand batters and also hurled fifty-six shutouts. He pitched his only no-hitter on August 14, 1971, against the Pirates. After struggling through the 1975 campaign on bad legs, Gibson decided in early September that it was time to retire when light-hitting Pete LaCock socked a grand-slam home run against him.

Brock played until 1979, each year adding more records to his career accomplishments. Most significantly, his 118 steals in 1974 shattered Maury Wills's single-season record of 104, set in 1962, and remained the major-league record until Rickey Henderson stole 130 bases in 1982. At age thirty-five in 1974, Brock was by far the oldest man to steal a hundred or more bases. "I figured it was now or never," he said. He dropped off to "only" 56 steals in each of the next two seasons, then dipped to a .221 batting average and 17 steals in 1978. Brock lost his regular job as the starter in left field and was urged to retire. Instead he rebounded the next season, batting .304 with 21 steals. He retired after the season, the all-time stolen-base leader with 938. Brock, like Gibson before him, was elected to the Hall of Fame in his first year of eligibility.

The Cardinals had a third future Hall of Famer in the early 1970s, but unfortunately for St. Louis, he did not remain with the team for long. Steve Carlton turned in a fine 17–11 record in 1969. After an off year in 1970, Carlton went 20–9 in 1971, but then he was unceremoniously traded to the Phillies for journeyman pitcher Rick Wise. Carlton did not like what he regarded as arbitrary player rules and tightfisted salaries, nor did he care for Gussie Busch's personality. In Philadelphia he blossomed into the best pitcher of the 1970s, chalking up five additional twenty-win seasons on his way to a 329–244 lifetime record and guiding the Phillies to a string of postseason appearances. Carlton's most remarkable season was 1972, when he went 27–10 for a Phillies team that won only 59 games and finished last in the National League East.

Seven other players came to the Cardinals in the first half of the 1970s to excite fans, even if the team won no championships. The first was Joe Torre, whom the Braves traded to the Cardinals straight up for former Most Valuable Player Orlando Cepeda at the end of the 1968 season. Torre drove in more than one hundred runs in each of the next three seasons. He filled Cepeda's spot at first base, then briefly replaced Tim McCarver behind the plate after McCarver was dealt to the Phillies in 1970, but was moved to third base in midseason when Mike Shannon was sidelined by a career-ending illness. Torre's .325 average and 21 home runs in 1970 was topped the next season when he led the National League in total bases (352) and hits (230) in addition to batting .363, driving in 137 runs, and belting 24 homers. He fully deserved the Most Valuable Player award he received that year. Torre hit in the .280s for the next three seasons but saw his power drop. In 1974 he went to the Mets; he retired as a player in 1977 to become the Mets' manager.

The second significant impact player of the era was Richie Allen, who informed everyone that he wished to be called "Dick" after his trade from the

Phillies to the Cards. The talented and troublesome Allen played in St. Louis for only one season—1970—but popped 34 home runs and drove in 101 runs at pitcher-friendly Busch Stadium. Allen gave his best on the field, everyone agreed, but his outspoken politics and his lackadaisical attitude toward meeting buses and airplanes on time ensured that he ran general managers ragged. He played for four different teams in four different years between 1969 and 1972, a record emblematic of his problem status. Jim Bouton voiced the perspective of Allen's fellow players, however, when he commented in *Ball Four* that Allen should be able to do what he wanted. "If I could get Allen I'd grab him and tell everybody that he marches to a different drummer, and that there are rules for him and different rules for everybody else. I mean," Bouton added, "what's the good of a .220 hitter who obeys the curfew? Richie Allen doesn't obey the rules, hits 35 home runs and knocks in over 100. I'll take him."

The third significant player, Ken Reitz, came up from the minors in 1973 to take over at third base. An excellent glove man, Reitz led National League third basemen in fielding percentage in each of his first two seasons and captured a Gold Glove in 1975. His nine errors in 1977 were the fewest ever at third base in league history, and he bettered that mark by committing just eight miscues in 1980. A handsome figure with long, dark hair, Reitz was with the Cardinals from 1972 to 1980, except for 1976, which he spent in San Francisco. A consistent yet unspectacular hitter, in 1977 he smashed seventeen homers, by far his greatest show of power.

Fourth, second baseman Ted Sizemore went to St. Louis in a trade for Dick Allen following the 1970 season. Lou Brock credited Sizemore with helping him break Wills's stolen-base record in 1974. "You have to have the right man batting behind you," said Brock. "I do. Ted Sizemore. He has to be unselfish, because hitting behind me isn't going to do any good for his batting average. He's going to be distracted by me instead of giving his complete concentration to the pitcher." Sizemore played for the Cardinals between 1971 and 1975 before moving to the Phillies, where he started at second on Philadelphia's 1977 and 1978 division championship teams.

Fifth, Keith Hernandez came up to the Cardinals to play first base in 1974 and soon established himself as the best-fielding first baseman of his time, winning eleven straight Gold Gloves and setting major-league records at first base for most seasons leading his league in double plays (six) and for lifetime assists. His great range helped him lead the National League at his position in assists five times, putouts four times, and fielding average twice.

Hernandez also hit well. He won a batting title in 1979 and was part of the only shared MVP award in history that year (Willie Stargell was the other recipient) as well as Player of the Year award. He had career highs with 48 doubles and 116 runs, both league-leading totals, and 105 RBIs. His .344 batting average, also a career high, marked the first time he had hit better than .300, but he went on to top .300 five other times. However, while with the Cardinals, he had a reputation as a carefree, undisciplined player.

The sixth significant player, Al Hrabosky, also known as "the Mad Hungarian," reached the Cardinals in 1970 as a left-handed relief pitcher. In essence a journeyman, Hrabosky was always entertaining. The chunky southpaw sported a bushy Fu Manchu mustache and long hair, and he dramatically stomped to the back of the mound to psyche himself up. His antics belied the fact that early in his career Hrabosky had a good fastball that enabled him to serve as a closer for the Cardinals. The fact that he used it 90 percent of the time proved his undoing as the hitters got used to seeing it, and its speed slowed as he aged. When he was not selected to the All-Star team in 1974, St. Louis fans rallied behind him, honoring him with a "We Hlove Hrabosky Hbanner Hday." Hrabosky's best year came in 1975, when he went 13–3 with a 1.67 ERA and 22 saves. The Cards traded him in December 1977 to the Royals for reliever Mark Littell, and in 1979 he signed a multi-million-dollar contract with the Braves via free agency, but recorded only seven saves with Atlanta (of his lifetime 97). He later became a Cardinals broadcaster, where his quirky dramatics proved an asset.

The Cardinals and the Counterculture Catcher

Finally, the most significant of the new Cardinals of the 1970s was Ted Simmons. "Simba," as he liked to be called, became an All-Star catcher soon after he took over as the Cardinals' starter in 1970. A true product of the 1960s counterculture, Simmons featured long locks and a stridently leftist political philosophy. He often played hurt and always played hard. Only average defensively, Simmons wreaked havoc on opposing pitchers when he came up to bat. Seven times he batted better than .300, six times reached 20 homers, and eight times exceeded 90 RBIs. He switch-hit home runs in a game three times and established the National League career record for home runs by a switch-hitter (182). Although not a threat to steal bases, Simmons had enough speed to amass 477 doubles.

Simmons had just turned nineteen when he played his first games for the Cardinals in 1968. A stocky six-footer from Highland Park, Michigan (near Detroit), Simmons had been an all-state high school fullback and earned a football scholarship from legendary coach Bo Schembechler at the University of Michigan. But he also played baseball, and the Cardinals drafted him number one in 1967, offering him a $50,000 signing bonus. Accordingly, he left the gridiron for the diamond. It proved an auspicious decision for Simmons, who was neither fast nor agile enough to play professional football as a running back and probably would have ended up as a linebacker with a career of less than a decade. Instead, he played in the major leagues for twenty-one seasons and went on to a front-office career after completing his playing days.

The Cardinals' brass knew they had a talented, intelligent, and sensitive young man on their hands in Simmons, a person who might attain superstar status. Manager Red Schoendienst carefully groomed Simmons to succeed the extremely popular and talented Tim McCarver, eventually dispatching McCarver to Philadelphia after the 1969 season to make room for the younger catcher. After annihilating minor-league pitching with power and average for three seasons, Simmons reached St. Louis to stay in 1970 and became the team's regular catcher for the next eleven years.

As Simmons made his way through the minor leagues in the late 1960s, he continued to take classes at the University of Michigan, and his experience in Ann Arbor had a catalytic influence on the rest of his life. The University of Michigan was one of the nation's most radical campuses, the place where the leftist Students for a Democratic Society had been founded and remained based. They were against the war in Vietnam, in favor of civil rights for African Americans, and in opposition to the status quo in the America of President Richard Nixon. A poet trapped in the body of a jock, Simmons drank in the revolutionary environment of the Michigan campus. He let his hair grow long like his idols of the left, rode a motorcycle like Peter Fonda in *Easy Rider,* and demonstrated with his classmates.

Most disturbing to the buttoned-down, corporate Cardinals front office, Simmons flaunted his individuality from the time of his appearance in St. Louis until his departure. He became a rebel in shinguards. Most of his teammates enjoyed what they thought of as his extravagant flakiness. Joe Torre called him "a flower child" with a broad grin. Simmons kept his flakiness, if not his long hair, for his entire career. It seemed totally in character for Simmons to admit in a postgame television interview that he had illegally blocked the plate during a close play at an All-Star game. According to the rules, Simmons announced, the catcher is not supposed to block the plate unless he has the ball, but sometimes "you just have to cheat." A collective belly laugh escaped across television land with that comment.

Almost immediately, Simmons ran afoul of the Cardinals over his contract. After batting .304 in 1971 and emerging as a star—but still making only $14,000 for the season—Simmons wanted a big raise in 1972. He did not make enough as a major leaguer to buy a house for his family and had to live with his wife's parents during the off-season. Simmons believed he deserved $30,000 in 1972, but General Manager Bing Devine offered him a contract that was in the low twenties. He refused to give Simmons a big contract too soon for fear of raising the mark for future negotiations; after all, Simmons would be a star for the Cards for a long time and presumably would receive raises every year. Simmons, displaying a bent learned at the University of Michigan, refused to accept Devine's verdict, arguing that his request for $30,000 did not even reach the league average of $34,000.

When Simmons could not reach a contract price with the Cardinals, he met with Marvin Miller of the Major League Players Association to discuss his options. Simmons decided to challenge the reserve clause by playing without a contract in 1972 and announcing his intention of becoming a free agent in 1973. He became the first major-league player to work without a valid contract when the 1972 season began. He recalled, "When someone representing the establishment said, 'This is what you'll do,' I was just bulletproof enough, naive enough, and political enough to say, 'I'm not going to.'" His stance placed the Cardinals in a very difficult position, and they took every possible tack in seeking to resolve the dispute except giving Simmons what he asked for and probably deserved.

As the season progressed with Simmons having a banner year behind the plate while playing without a contract, the owners got worried. Major League general counsel John Gaherin told Bing Devine, "Get a hold of this. We don't want to test [the reserve clause]. Sign him. Don't let him go through this year without a contract." August Busch put incredible pressure on Simmons to sign. One night he cornered Simmons in Red Schoendienst's office before a game and lectured him on duty, responsibility, and loyalty before offering him a contract in the high twenties. Busch threatened to cut Simmons's salary to the league minimum of $12,000 if he continued his belligerency. Simmons countered with a lecture of his own on duty, responsibility, and loyalty and suggested that Busch should have some toward his players, before telling the owner what he could do with his new offer. The first pitch of the game that night had to be held up until this tête-à-tête ended.

Simmons refused to budge in his demand for $30,000, and as the season wore into late June his well-publicized campaign gained adherents. He helped his cause with excellent on-field performances, hustling and always making the crucial play, or so it seemed to Cardinals fans. Many publicly announced that Simmons deserved his $30,000, and that Busch should give it to him. When Simmons gained an invitation to the All-Star game in July, the dispute reached a new level. Gaherin asserted that Major League Baseball had to settle this problem with Simmons, that a test of the reserve clause would only bring defeat to the owners and thereby allow players to move at will. "Fellas, this is the twentieth century," Gaherin explained. "You can't get anybody, drunk or sober, to agree that once a fella goes to work for the A&P, he has to work for the A&P the rest of his life."

The confrontation reached a climax the morning of the All-Star game in Atlanta. While preparing for the game, Simmons received a phone call from Bing Devine, who asked to meet with him about the contract dispute. When they met, Devine offered a two-year deal too good to pass up: $30,000 for 1972 and $45,000 for 1973. Before agreeing, Simmons went back to his room and called his wife: "Maryanne . . . here's what's happened. I've got to do this." He signed the contract on August 9, 1972. The Cardinals bought off a young and hungry player who needed the money to support his family. Seemingly, Miller and Simmons both recognized that the major-league owners would do almost anything to prevent a test of the reserve clause.

Simmons did not regret making the decision to sign this contract. It was the largest salary he had ever known, although he would later make more money per season than any other catcher except Cincinnati's Johnny Bench and Boston's Carlton Fisk. He continued to play mind games with the Cardinals management over contracts for the rest of his career. This made him something of a pariah in baseball management circles, but a big star among his colleagues.

His play on the field also won over most of the Cardinals fans. However, it failed to win over the new Cardinals manager, stern disciplinarian Vern Rapp, who replaced Red Schoendienst in 1977. Rapp's distinctly old-fashioned approach to his job did not sit well with Simmons and several other players. Rapp had no interest in providing free spirits an opportunity to excel, even calling Simmons a "loser." Simmons, a team leader among the players, constantly clashed with his new manager. Early in the 1978 season Rapp suffered what could only be called a mutiny in the clubhouse led by Simmons. Rapp lost and was replaced by Ken Boyer, who took a much more accepting approach toward dealing with his players.

But the next manager after Boyer, Whitey Herzog, had his own way of dealing with Simmons and a lot of other Cardinals players who had their own perspective on the world. Herzog sent Simmons to the Milwaukee Brewers for the 1981 season. The clubhouse was not big enough for both of them. In Milwaukee, Simmons helped the Brewers win the second-half American League East title in the strike-split 1981 season and hit a crucial two-run homer in Game Three of the division playoff as the Brewers temporarily staved off elimination. In 1982 he led Milwaukee all the way to the World Series—against his former team. Simmons hit for a poor average in the postseason, but he did smack home runs in the first two games of the World Series against the Cardinals. His greatest clutch performance may have come in 1983, when he drove in 108 runs with only 13 homers. He closed out his career during 1986–1988 as a member of the Braves' self-dubbed "Bomb Squad" of utility specialists, playing first base, catcher, and third base, and serving as a valued pinch-hitter. In October 1988, Simmons was hired by General Manager Dal Maxvill, a former teammate, to be the Cardinals' director of player development.

The White Rat Comes to St. Louis

It did not take Whitey Herzog long to rebuild the St. Louis Cardinals into a team in his own image once he arrived in 1980. In early June the Cards were stumbling to an 18–53 record, and Ken Boyer lost his job. Herzog took over a team that hit well, averaging .275, but did not have any pitching worth talking about. As both general manager and field manager, Herzog emphasized his "Whiteyball" style of play on the field—pitching, speed, and defense—the hallmark of the great Cardinals teams of the past. In his autobiography, *White Rat,* Herzog explained his reasoning on why a team built on these traits could win in the National League: "In baseball today, geography is all-important. In the National League, you've got a whole bunch of big ballparks—ten to be exact— where it's hard to hit home runs. Our park in St. Louis, where we play eighty-one games a year, is the toughest hitter's park of them all."

Since this was the case, Herzog began looking for solid pitchers and swift runners who could handle a glove. He knew how to judge talent. Herzog had been both a scout and director of player development for successful teams, and he immediately made useful acquisitions. On December 8, 1980, he acquired from the San Diego Padres two key players, relief ace Rollie Fingers and catcher Gene Tenace. The next day he acquired perhaps the best closing pitcher in baseball, Bruce Sutter, from the Chicago Cubs. Having Fingers and Sutter in the same bullpen presented some difficulties, for both pitchers expected to be called upon in "save" opportunities. Keeping them both happy would be impossible, and Herzog decided to use one as trade bait. As a result, on December 12 Herzog dealt Fingers to Milwaukee along with Simmons and starting pitcher Pete Vukovich in return for speed-burning outfielders Sixto Lezcano and David Green and pitchers Lary Sorensen and Dave LaPoint. He then signed veteran catcher Darrell Porter, who had worked with him in Kansas City, to take over behind the plate. In less than a week Herzog had remade the team in his own image, unloading thirteen players and adding nine.

The Cardinals immediately responded to these changes on the field. In the strike-shortened 1981 season, when the middle third of the season was lost because of a fully legitimate players' strike to prevent the owners from rolling back hard-won benefits, the Cards had the best record in the National League East,

The 1982 World Champion Cardinals. Courtesy of Classicphotos.com, Ely, Minnesota.

59–43. Unfortunately, because of the strike, the owners decided to divide the season into two parts and to have the winner of each half meet in a playoff to determine the division champion. The Cardinals were one-and-a-half games behind Philadelphia when the strike began and therefore failed to win that half. They then trailed the second-half winner, the Montreal Expos, by a half game. As a result, they sat out the postseason, along with the Cincinnati Reds, who had the best overall record in the National League but failed to win the West division outright in either half of the season. With the two best teams in the National League failing to make the playoffs, the Los Angeles Dodgers went to the World Series and defeated the Yankees for the championship.

Winning It All—1982

In 1982, the Cardinals roared to the division championship, the National League pennant, and victory in the World Series. It was the Cardinals' first World Championship since "El Birdos" of 1967 and their first appearance in the postseason since 1968. Herzog built on his earlier success by acquiring in the fall of 1981 several key pieces to the championship team of 1982. The first move took place on October 21, 1981, and turned out better than anyone would have expected. A young minor leaguer named Willie McGee was acquired from the

Yankees for an also-ran pitcher. McGee immediately took over in center field. A bad-ball hitter who might swing at anything thrown, McGee succeeded year after year. In 1982 he hit .292 to spur the Cardinals' offense. In his best year, 1985, McGee hit .353 and won the first of his two batting titles. His average was the highest in history for a switch-hitter. In 1987, now hitting behind Jack Clark, he led the National League in on-base percentage and drove in a career-high 105 runs. A speed-burner, McGee was always a threat to steal bases, and he had enormous range in center field.

Herzog also acquired speedy outfielder Lonnie Smith from the Cleveland Indians in November 1981. In Smith and McGee, the Cardinals had two players who could cover a lot of ground in the spacious Busch Stadium outfield and manufacture runs with their speed on the base paths. Indeed, Herzog told the St. Louis fans during spring training in 1982 that while he did not expect the Cardinals to hit many home runs, he guaranteed that there would always be some "jackrabbits" on base at the top of the order for the RBI producers to drive in.

By far Herzog's most significant acquisition took place on February 11, 1982, when he obtained Ozzie Smith from the San Diego Padres in a swap of shortstops. The trade of Garry Templeton for Ozzie Smith ranks as one of the best in Cardinals history, close behind the Lou Brock acquisition. No question about it, the "Wizard of Oz," or "The Wizard of Ah!'s," as he came to be called in St. Louis, was the greatest glove man at shortstop in baseball history. For nineteen years, Ozzie Smith dominated baseball with breathtaking and often game-saving defensive play. To watch him play was to see a combination of baseball, acrobatics, ballet, and gymnastics. Beginning in 1980, Smith won thirteen straight Gold Gloves at shortstop and led the National League in fielding percentage seven times. Herzog knew well what he had in Ozzie Smith. "Ozzie is not only the greatest defensive shortstop ever to play the game, but he's also a first-rate human being, a leader in the best sense of the word." Those leadership qualities alone were worth the price, as Smith filled a void in the clubhouse. Herzog argued that at his peak Smith saved seventy-five runs per year with his glove, and that was probably a conservative estimate. Smith fully deserved the first million-dollar shortstop contract, which he received from the Cardinals on January 19, 1983, when he signed a three-year deal with the team.

Smith played three years in San Diego between 1978 and 1981, but the Padres were willing to give up on him because they questioned his offensive abilities. The Cardinals did not necessarily need his offense, although he later turned into an adequate hitter, because he provided such a critical piece to the Cardinals' quest for a strong defense up the middle. With second baseman Tom Herr (also a good glove man), Willie McGee in center field, and sure-handed Darrell Porter behind the plate, the Cardinals had one of the strongest middle defenses in baseball in the 1980s. Because they rarely scored many runs and almost never routed an opponent, they relied heavily on Smith's ability to thwart late-inning hits. It was a highly successful formula in the 1980s.

Smith's batting also improved as he gained confidence and experience. The switch-hitting Smith posted a .276 batting average in 1985, improved to .280 in 1986, then hit a career-high .303 in 1987 with 43 stolen bases, 75 RBIs, and 104 runs scored. When Smith announced that 1996 would be his last season, a special effort was made to let him, by then platooning with Royce Clayton, play in each National League park as a farewell to hordes of adoring fans throughout the country. In his first year of eligibility to be elected to the Hall of Fame, Ozzie Smith will surely join other Cardinals superstars in Cooperstown.

Ozzie Smith also excelled at a tradition in St. Louis, started by Stan Musial and continued by Lou Brock and other star Cardinals, of gentlemanly involvement in the community. Smith made St. Louis his permanent home and worked to make it a better place. For these efforts he received both the Branch Rickey Award in 1994 and the Roberto Clemente Award in 1995. With his playing days behind him, Smith remains a powerful force in St. Louis, involved in both business and civic activities.

Fire-balling right-handed pitcher Joaquin Andujar was the last piece of the puzzle for the team that won the pennant in 1982. Referring to himself as "one tough Dominican," the colorful Andujar reached his peak in the mid-1980s as a workhorse who pitched well on three days' rest. Coming over during the 1981 season from the Houston Astros, a team that had not been able to handle his unique personality and had misused him in the bullpen, Andujar's 15–10 record and 2.47 earned run average in 1982 helped St. Louis to the World Championship. His 20–14 record in 1984 was a true bright spot for the Cardinals pitching staff, and in 1985 his 21–12 record matched well with left-hander John Tudor's 21–8 mark.

The Cardinals popped out of the gate quickly in the spring of 1982 and took the National League East title without much difficulty by finishing with a 92–70 record, three games ahead of the Phillies. Consistency ensured their success, as the team lost no more than three games in a row at any time during the season. Herzog's team, true to his predictions, hit a mere sixty-seven home runs for the season, leading him to quip that he feared that his Cardinals would not even match Roger Maris's sixty-one homers in 1961. The Cardinals were last in the major leagues in home runs, and they were the first team to win a division title with such a poor home run total. But they produced runs by speed, stealing more than two hundred bases, and their strong pitching and defense ensured that the opposition did not score often. Andujar and Bob Forsch (15–9) led a lackluster rotation of starting pitchers that did just well enough to win. But key to the team's success was bullpen ace Bruce Sutter, who won nine and saved a league-leading 36 games.

In the playoffs the Cardinals met the Atlanta Braves, winners of the National League West, to determine who would go to the World Series. It was more like a public execution than a playoff. The Braves, making their first postseason appearance since 1969, were swept in three straight games. Despite leading the National League in homers and runs, Atlanta scored only five times against the Cardinals in the series. Fate played a hand in the sweep as rain washed out the opener two outs shy of an official Braves victory. It was the first rain-out at Busch Stadium since 1976. St. Louis beat the Braves bombers 7–0, 4–3, and 6–2 to reach the World Series, where they played the Milwaukee Brewers. It was the first trip for the Brewers to the series, and they made it in no small measure because of Herzog's trades of Ted Simmons, Rollie Fingers, and Pete Vukovich there. All three players had proved enormously influential in leading the Brewers to the postseason.

Under manager Harvey Kuenn, the Brewers, nicknamed "Harvey's Wall-bangers" for blasting 216 homers, the most in the majors in eighteen years, could not hold a three-games-to-two series edge against the team that hit the fewest homers of anyone. In the end the Cardinals won their ninth World Series after beating Milwaukee in Games Six and Seven. Because of his timely hitting and defense, catcher Darrell Porter received the MVP award, posting a .286 average with five RBIs. Cardinals outfielder Dane Iorg batted .529, while first baseman Keith Hernandez drove in nine runs. Most important, Joaquin Andujar finished 2–0 with a 1.35 ERA for the series.

The series started off badly for the Cardinals, as Milwaukee pounded them 10–0 in Busch Stadium. But the Cards came back to take the second and third games 5–4 and 6–2. In the third game Willie McGee put on a hitting display that made the "wallbangers" flinch, slugging two home runs in the game. The feat was all the more remarkable because he had hit only four homers all season. Milwaukee then took the next two games, 7–5 and 6–4, setting up a "do or die" scenario for the Cardinals. They beat the Brewers 13–1 in Game Six to tie the series. Only one team, the Detroit Tigers in 1968, had previously been able to beat the Cardinals in a seven-game World Series. Possessing a 6–1 record in series finales, St. Louis rallied from a 3–1 deficit in the sixth inning of the seventh game to put away the Brewers. When it was over, series MVP Darrell Porter sized it up like this: "H-o-o-i-e, I've been to two country fairs and a goat roast—and I ain't never seen nuthin' like this." Porter was not far off; it was a great World Series.

For Whitey Herzog, who had been unable to bring a pennant to Kansas City despite leading an aggressive young Royals team to three division titles, the 1982

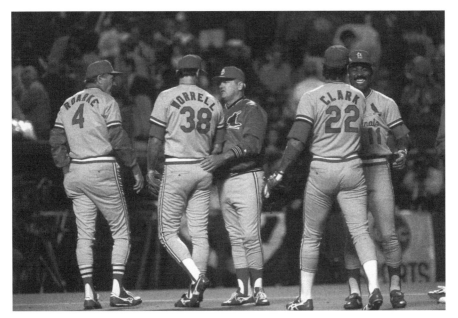

The Cardinals were one of the best teams in the National League throughout the 1980s, winning three pennants and one World Series. (Courtesy of the Kansas City Royals.)

World Series victory proved especially satisfying. He no longer had to listen to castigation for "choking" in the playoffs. And his philosophy of strong pitching, speed, and defense gained even greater currency after the Cards beat the powerhouse Braves and Brewers en route to the championship. Other teams tried to emulate his approach, but they had decidedly mixed success.

But winning in 1982 made the Cardinals complacent. In 1983 the team slumped to fourth in the division. Halfway through the season, Herzog started to make changes to his team. The most important took place on June 15 when he traded Keith Hernandez to the last-place Mets for journeyman relief pitchers Neil Allen and Rick Ownbey. The trade came as a shock to Cardinals fans, for Hernandez was immensely popular in St. Louis and his play on the field was unparalleled in the National League. Everyone pointed to him as the exemplar of the best there was at first base.

Herzog took enormous heat for the Hernandez trade, especially because of its seemingly unequal nature, and he defended himself by saying that the Cardinals needed good pitching and that Allen and Ownbey would be huge additions. They weren't, of course, but his argument masked a deeper concern. Herzog thought Hernandez had an "attitude problem" that kept him from giving 100 percent on the field. And Herzog said so. He also suspected that Hernandez was using drugs. When Herzog further defended the trade by leaking that story to the media, Hernandez threatened a libel suit, but the 1985 Pittsburgh drug trials revealed it to be true. Hernandez went on to star with the Mets during their 1986 championship season and then retired in 1990 after a stellar seventeen-year career.

The Cardinals never recovered their stellar level of play from the previous season. In fact, the 1983 team was every bit as inconsistent as the 1982 champions had been steady. Eight-game losing streaks in both June and August and a seven-game losing streak in September plunged the team to the bottom of the standings. In the end the Cardinals finished 79–83 for the season, a distant fourth in the National League East. The 1984 version of the Cardinals was better but still finished only 84–78, third in the division. Andujar won 20 games, but the team lost closer Bruce Sutter, who led the league with 45 saves in 1984, to free agency at the end of the season. Sutter's departure especially troubled Herzog, who commented, "My whole team was the preliminary act to Bruce Sutter's show-stopper, and the world knew it."

The I-70 Series

Almost no one picked the Cardinals to win the National League pennant in 1985. But the fact is that they did, and they came close to beating the Kansas City Royals in one of the best seven-game World Series ever. This resulted in no small measure from the field leadership of Whitey Herzog, whose management style many analysts concluded added seven to nine wins to any team's total for a season. A swing in victories on that scale is usually enough to move a team from the second division to first place. That seems to have been the case in 1985 for the Cardinals. Herzog got excellent performances from a talented bunch of "jackrabbits," as he liked to call his swift starting lineup, and superb pitching performances from three starters: Joaquin Andujar, who went 21–12, left-hander John Tudor (21–8, with 10 shutouts), and Danny Cox (18–9). Most especially, Herzog oversaw a "bullpen by committee" that was worthy of following in Sutter's footsteps. With four different closers, this committee managed forty-four saves, only one less than Sutter had compiled the year before. Late in the season Herzog brought fireballing right-hander Todd Worrell up from the minors, and Worrell quickly took over the stopper role. The bullpen pitchers got the job done; the Cardinals were 83–1 in games that they led after seven innings. In 1985 they simply did not blow leads.

Herzog's "jackrabbits" demonstrated in 1985 a most effective scratch-run offense that rivaled anything seen before in Cardinals history. Five of the starters were switch-hitters, eliminating the necessity of platooning players based on whether or not lefties or right-handers were on the mound and taking away the ability of opposing managers to make pitching changes based on whether a batter was left-handed or right-handed. Led by Willie McGee and his .353 batting average, the offense scorched the ball all season for a league-leading .264 team average. The fleet outfield of McGee, Vince Coleman (who took Rookie of the Year honors), and Andy Van Slyke nailed down everything that came to them. The infield of Terry Pendleton at third, Ozzie Smith at shortstop, Tom Herr at second, and Jack Clark at first provided excellent defense as well. The team's .983 fielding percentage was the best in the National League and one of the greatest defensive displays in Cardinals history. Pendleton, Van Slyke, and Coleman, all recent call-ups to the majors, emerged in 1985 as stars. One story about Coleman, indicative perhaps of his naïveté, was his response to the question, what did he think was the legacy of Jackie Robinson? Coleman looked puzzled and said, "Who's he?" Clark came to the Cardinals before the season as a castoff from the Giants and soon proved his mettle as the team's clean-up hitter.

These players were really fast, and showed it in every game. They stole a team-record 314 bases, in the process exasperating the opposition and winning games in the resulting confusion. Vince Coleman stole 110 bases for the season, leading both the team and the league. Willie McGee swiped an additional 56, and Herr, Van Slyke, and Ozzie Smith each had more than 30. If they had traded in their baseball double-knits for sleek track suits, they could have taken gold medals at the Olympics. All they needed was a torch.

The Cardinals won 101 games in 1985 while losing only 61, a .623 winning percentage that was the best in the majors. Only the 1931, 1942–1944, and 1967 Cardinals teams equaled them in victories. They then met the Los Angeles Dodgers in a best-of-seven league championship series. It seemed like the Cards would certainly have trouble with the Dodgers, the winners of the National League West, especially when the team lost the first two games in Los Angeles.

Disaster struck again when the playoffs resumed in St. Louis for Game Three. Before the game started the fastest "jackrabbit," Vince Coleman, was lost for the remainder of the postseason in one of the strangest accidents in baseball history. The automatic tarpaulin that covered the infield at Busch Memorial Stadium, moving at less than one mile per hour to cover the field during a rain delay, still managed to trap the speedster's ankle. While suffering nothing more serious than bruises, Coleman's injury seemed to foreshadow a bizarre postseason.

The wittiest news story about the Dodgers-Cardinals series came from Mike Lupica of the *New York Daily News* who wrote under the headline, "The World

According to Tarp." In Game Three, however, St. Louis did not miss its lead-off hitter and proved it by scoring a series-record nine runs in the second inning. The Cardinals then proceeded to win Game Four and, in dramatic fashion, Game Five as well on an Ozzie Smith home run in the bottom of the ninth. "Go crazy, folks! Go crazy!" That was Cardinals' announcer Jack Buck's call. The series went back to Los Angeles for Game Six with the Dodgers suddenly on the brink of elimination.

If the Cardinals won Game Six, they would go on to their fourteenth World Series; if they lost, the Dodgers lived to play a seventh and deciding game. In that sixth game, the Dodgers beat themselves, electing to pitch to slugger Jack Clark with two outs in the ninth and the Cardinals behind by a run, 5–4. First base was open, but Cardinals were on second and third, and those in the stands heaved a collective gasp when Clark did not receive an intentional walk. Clark loved situations like that, and he homered to beat the Dodgers, 7–5.

Overall, shortstop Ozzie Smith stole the spotlight, winning series MVP honors by batting .435, hitting his dramatic game-winning home run—his first left-handed homer in nearly 3,000 at bats—and tying Game Six with a seventh-inning triple. All summer Smith had suffered from bad press over his much-ballyhooed contract of two million dollars a year. Labor problems had plagued the game since the 1981 midseason strike, and many of the owners were mounting a campaign—of course it was nonspecific as to culprits—against players who were greedy, overpaid, underworked, and forcing teams into bankruptcy. Nothing could have been further from the truth, but it made good copy and accordingly many sports journalists took the bait; they, of course, did not blanch from naming culprits. One target was Smith and his salary, which many considered ridiculous for a lifetime .238 hitter.

Whitey Herzog and the Cardinals front office did not agree. Ozzie the acrobat sucked up ground balls all over the left side of the infield, and with the artificial turf and distant fences of Busch Stadium a great glove was better than a slugger any day of the week. After Smith's astounding performance in the playoffs, however, *Newsweek* reporter Pete Axthelm reached an eminently fair conclusion. "Measured against current salaries, Smith's is fair. Measured by last week's surprises, he's underpaid. His unique homer won game five and his triple kept the Cards in game six until Clark's homer could win it." The irrepressible Dodgers manager Tommy Lasorda gave Smith the quintessential compliment when he said of his performance, "I'm dumbstruck."

Meanwhile, in the American League, were it not for the expansion of the League Championship Series to a best-of-seven format, the Toronto Blue Jays, winners of the East division, would have taken the pennant. But after winning three of the first four games, the Blue Jays lost their steam and Kansas City swept the last three games to take their second pennant in six years. Not surprisingly, George Brett ignited Kansas City's offense. His four hits in Game Three (including two home runs) gave the club its first victory, and his RBI ground-out in Game Five and go-ahead homer in Game Six proved game-winners in contests the Royals had to win. Despite a regular-season record of only ninety-one wins, barely enough to survive a resurgent California Angels team, the Royals showed the mettle that would bring them ultimate victory.

In fact, one could almost trace the return of the Royals to excellence from two incidents in the 1983 season. One took place on July 25, and has gone down in the annals of baseball history as the "Pine Tar Incident." The incident remains classic footage to this day: an enraged Brett charging out of the dugout toward Tim McClelland after the rookie umpire disallowed a two-run homer off Yankee closer Rich "Goose" Gossage that would have given the Royals a 5–4 lead in the top of the ninth inning. Yankee manager Billy Martin quickly protested to McClelland, citing the amount of pine tar Brett had applied to his bat. "You gotta call him out, pal," Martin told McClelland, "you gotta call him out."

McClelland consulted with the other umpires before measuring the bat. According to the rules, pine tar could not exceed seventeen inches on the grip end of the bat. "When we measured it, the pine tar was a good seven or eight inches farther," McClelland recalled, "and I knew then we had a problem." He called Brett out, and the Royals great went from euphoria to rage in an instant. Brett admitted that never before had he been so mad. "I'd been frustrated before," Brett said. "You're frustrated that you . . . made an error that let in two or three runs and we ended up losing the game by one or two runs. That's frustration. That's not mad." Brett was incredulous that the umpires would enforce such a rule, and then his incredulity turned to stark red-eyed anger. Brett commented, "When they put the bat on the ground, to measure it against home plate, someone said, 'They're measuring the bat against the plate to see how much pine tar you have on it.' . . . And I said, 'If they call me out for that, they're in trouble.' "

Brett had to be tackled and held down from attacking McClelland. He blistered McClelland with every epithet he knew, and every player knows many. The video of the game became the standard on television for the rest of the season and periodically thereafter. Lip readers enjoyed picking out Brett's phrases, and manager Dick Howser had to protect his greatest player while both teams' benches emptied. All the while, the paranoid and brilliant Billy Martin stood off to the side and let the Royals self-destruct. That night, McClelland stumbled across the entire Royals team in the airport. Acting the gentleman, he walked up to Brett and tried to make amends. "You're not really that mad at me, are you?" Brett responded, "You're [darn] right I am." To this day, Brett believes that McClelland should not have enforced the pine tar rule.

Dick Howser protested the call and the game, and American League President Lee McPhail, "in the spirit of the rules," finally allowed the home run on appeal. Out of the whole mess, one irony was not lost on McClelland. "George Brett was probably, and I think most umpires would tell you this, one of the best players to umpires that there's been in the game," he said. "George was always joking, always having fun." He was a gentleman every other time they met, but he was truly angry at the petty ruling. McClelland was ever after known as "The Pine-Tar Umpire." Martin also lost the Yankee advantage they had once enjoyed over the Royals. It made them all the more competitive every time they met. Through the crucible of the Pine Tar Incident, an injured Brett emerged in 1984 to lead the Royals to their first division title since 1980. This set the stage for the 1985 world championship season.

The second incident during the Royals' 1983 season was ultimately more serious. In midsummer the team was rocked by a drug scandal involving Willie Wilson, Willie Aikens, Jerry Martin, and Vida Blue. These players pled guilty to charges of soliciting cocaine and received five-thousand-dollar fines and one-year prison terms, reduced to three months for good behavior. Baseball's commissioner, Bowie Kuhn, then suspended them for the 1984 season, but the Major League Baseball Players' Association protested, and Wilson, Martin, and a little while later Aiken were reinstated, although Blue remained under suspension for the entire year. The crisis tested the Royals both as a major-league franchise and as individuals. The soul-searching prompted serious reconsiderations of all aspects of their lives and activities. Despite the trial, they were better for having dealt with it.

The victories of the Cardinals and the Royals in their respective league playoffs in 1985 set up an all-Missouri championship meeting in what has been appropriately labeled the "I-70 Series," named for the interstate highway that connects the two great Missouri cities. None of the television moguls who purchased broadcast rights for the World Series were thrilled that Kansas City and St. Louis played each other in 1985. Both were relatively small markets and did not have the glamour of a New York or a Los Angeles. But the series attracted good television audiences, largely because it brought to the fore a widespread sympathy for two underdogs who came from behind to win their league championships. It also showcased the lovely cities of Kansas City and St. Louis and the teams that emulated the simple virtues of the quiet folks who lived there. Many people identified with these teams and their uniquely American values. Neither team was loaded with high-priced superstars—although there were well-paid stars on both teams—and each put forth an image of hard-working, team-oriented players that reflected considerable warmth. Neither team could win consistently with brute force, and that also attracted supporters. Instead, as Pete Axthelm reported, "The Mr. Octobers of this season have traded lusty slugging for elegance and acrobatics. The Show Me State is putting on a pretty good show."

The World Series started off well for the Cardinals, who took the first two games in Kansas City. In Game One, after the Royals took the lead with a run off lefty John Tudor (21–8) in the second inning, the St. Louis starter settled down to pitch well while the best defense in the National League made him look even better. The Cardinals caught Darryl Motley in a rundown between third and home in the second inning, preventing what might have become a big inning for the Royals. In the fourth, pitching with a 2–1 lead, Tudor escaped on an inning-ending double play. Tudor then held off the Royals until the seventh inning, in time for closer Todd Worrell to nail down the victory. The Cardinals got their runs off Royals starter Danny Jackson on Willie McGee's third-inning ground-out, Tito Landrum's and Cesar Cedeno's back-to-back doubles in the fourth, and Jack Clark's ninth-inning double. The game ended in a 3–1 win for the Cards over the Royals.

Cardinals shortstop Ozzie Smith throws out Royals center fielder Willie Wilson in the 1985 World Series. Courtesy of the Kansas City Royals Baseball Club.

In Game Two it looked as if the Royals might come back to even the series. Left-handed starter Charlie Leibrandt pitched magnificently for the first eight innings, allowing only two harmless singles and a walk, retiring twenty-four of twenty-seven Cardinals hitters. He also led in the game 2–0 thanks to back-to-back RBI doubles from George Brett and Frank White. But in the ninth, Leibrandt could not get the final out. Two outs after Willie McGee's lead-off double, Jack Clark singled for the first run, making the score 2–1 and putting the tying run on base. Tito Landrum then doubled, and Cesar Cedeno drew an intentional walk to load the bases. Terry Pendleton then chased home three runs with a double for a 4–2 lead. The St. Louis bullpen sealed the victory in the bottom of the ninth by mowing down the Royals, three up, three down.

With Cardinals victories in the first two games, most observers thought that a world championship was once again St. Louis–bound. Sportswriters commented on the dominance of the Cardinals as one of the greatest teams of all time. They concentrated on the excellent pitching staff with its two twenty-game winners, the speed-burning lineup of switch-hitters and base-stealers, and the defense that let nothing get through. Some suggested that the caliber of defense played by the Cardinals had not been seen in the World Series since 1970 when Baltimore Orioles third baseman Brooks Robinson put on a one-man fielding clinic to enable Baltimore's victory over a dominating Cincinnati Reds team with four future Hall of Famers. The poor Kansas City Royals, gallant though they might be, were simply overmatched by a great Cardinals team.

The sports reporters also turned their attention to the local flavor of Missouri, showcasing the culture of Middle America and celebrating the state's centrality to the best that the nation holds dear. "Much of the charm of the I-70 World Series lay on Missouri's back roads," reported Craig Neff in the October 28, 1985, issue of *Sports Illustrated*. Sent in search of local color, Neff found it everywhere. He stopped at the Midway–Locust Grove Methodist Church for its country ham dinner and found everyone talking baseball. There were fans dressed in Cardinals red and others wearing Royals blue, but they sat side by side peacefully debating the series. They disagreed over who would win, but it was always good-natured disagreement. Written on a chalkboard at the church were words that said much about how everyone viewed the series: "WE SUPPORT THE ST. KANSLOU CITY ROYINALS IN THE WORLD SERIES."

Halfway between St. Louis and Kansas City, on the University of Missouri campus in Columbia, Neff found the students excited about the series. The young men in the Pi Kappa Phi fraternity rallied behind two of their frat brothers, one from St. Louis and the other from Kansas City, to support either the

Cardinals or the Royals in the World Series. They wrote a little jingle about the friendly rivalry:

> It's brother against brother like the Civil War
> If you're from the opposition I ain't opening the door.

They divided their frat house down the middle, using masking tape to mark off the Cardinals supporters' section of the house from that controlled by the Royals supporters. Again, it was not serious, never engendering the kind of hatred seen in New York during the legendary battles between the Yankees, Dodgers, and Giants.

Perhaps best of all, in the middle of the state someone erected a sign across I-70 with two different statements, depending on whether one was traveling east or west. For motorists heading east from Kansas City to St. Louis, the sentiment read, "To *Hell* with Cosell, Go Royals!" For westbound travelers heading for Kansas City from St. Louis, the sign read, "To *Hell* with Cosell, Go Cards." In such a setting, only Howard Cosell seemed to suffer. Howard Cosell, of course, was the opinionated, arrogant, and by 1985 totally unloved broadcaster for ABC television network sports.

When the series resumed in St. Louis for Game Three, the Royals realized that their backs were to the wall. Signs in Busch Memorial Stadium expressed sentiments such as "The Fat Lady May Not Be Singing Yet, but She's Warming Up" and "It may not be over 'til its over, but Yogi was an optimist." Cardinals' fans believed their team would put the Royals away quickly, if not in four straight then at least during the three games scheduled for St. Louis. But both teams' loyal rooters were gracious toward their opponents, and everyone commented on the genuine joy that this World Series seemed to conjure up, with the players on both squads enjoying the friendly rivalry and the packed stadiums rocked with friendly competition. "Across the state," Tom Callahan reported in *Time,* "everyone decked out in red or blue appeared to have a touch or at least a tolerance of the other color." The graciousness of both sides forced one to conclude that, in contrast to some earlier World Series, this one might just as easily be called the "Series of Good Feelings" as the "I-70 Series." Never had the state of Missouri had such an opportunity to showcase its particular charisma, and few who visited there for the first time were disappointed.

In Game Three the Royals began to climb out of the hole they had dug in Kansas City. The staff's ace, right-handed twenty-game-winner Bret Saberhagen, the youngest World Series starter since Jim Palmer in 1966, tossed a masterful six-hitter. After allowing a sixth-inning run, the twenty-one-year-old hurler retired the final eleven Cardinals to come to the plate. Kansas City favorite son Frank White took top honors for run production, driving in three runs. Most spectacularly, the second baseman jacked a two-run homer out of Busch Stadium in the fifth inning. That was all that was needed to beat Cards' starter Joaquin Andujar, 6–1.

John Tudor came back in Game Four to shut out the Royals 3–0 with the kind of masterful performance not seen since the renowned efforts of Bob Gibson in the World Series in 1968. Backed by solo homers from Tito Landrum and Willie McGee, and by Tom Nieto's squeeze bunt, Tudor scattered five hits and struck out eight Royals, retiring thirteen consecutive hitters during one span as the Cardinals took a 3–1 series advantage. It looked like it would all be over in five games.

Such was not to be, however. Danny Jackson took the mound for the Royals in Game Five and pitched well, building a 4–0 lead after two innings. The Cardinals' starter, right-hander Bob Forsch, and reliever Todd Worrell struck out thirteen Royals between them, but could not seal a victory. In the end, the Royals won decisively, 6–1, setting up another "do or die" situation in the sixth game.

Game Six of the 1985 World Series has to go down as one of the most bizarre in the history of the postseason. Replayed over and over again, it still spells collapse for the Cardinals. The Royals won it by the narrowest of margins, 2–1, forcing a seventh game. But it was the process of getting to the 2–1 finale that made the game so strange. It was a classic pitcher's battle for seven innings as neither the Royals nor the Cardinals could do anything offensively. Cardinals starter Danny Cox and Royals hurler Charlie Liebrandt matched each other perfectly until the top of the eighth, when Cardinals pinch-hitter Brian Harper blooped a single to center to score Terry Pendleton. With the quality of the Cardinals bullpen, the 1–0 lead should probably have been enough to win the game and the series. But in the ninth inning the wheels came off the Cardinals' bandwagon.

Closer Todd Worrell came in to finish off the Royals in the bottom of the ninth. The first batter was pinch-hitter Jorge Orta, who hit a weak grounder to first baseman Jack Clark. Clark fielded it cleanly and flipped it to Worrell, who covered first from the pitcher's mound. In one of the worst calls in World Series play, first base umpire Don Denkinger called Orta safe. Replays on television and in Royals Stadium clearly showed that Orta had been beaten to first and should have been back on the Royals' bench. Whitey Herzog ran out to protest the call but failed to convince Denkinger to change his mind. In hindsight Herzog believed that he should have walked over to the box of baseball commissioner Peter Ueberroth and demanded that the umpiring team look at the replay. Had the commissioner refused, Herzog said he should then have pulled his team off the field in protest of what was clearly a bad call. In that case, Herzog said, "I'd have been right, but I'd have been fired." But he thinks Ueberroth would have acceded to his demand, and the replay would have forced a change in the call.

The bad call rattled the Cardinals beyond all hope of recovery. Forced to hold Orta on first, Jack Clark chased a pop foul from the bat of Steve Balboni to the home dugout, but lost it because of the weird angle and failed to make the catch. Balboni, who looked a little like Archie Bunker's son-in-law on *All in the Family,* only slower, then surprised everyone with a bloop single to put Royals at first and second with no outs. The Cards got Orta at third when Royals catcher Jim Sundberg failed in a sacrifice attempt, but then the base-runners reached second and third on a passed ball from catcher Darrell Porter. Hal McRae came to the plate with one out and runners in scoring position. McRae was always a danger-ous hitter, but he had been essentially nullified since the designated hitter was not used in this World Series. The Cards decided to walk him to get to another pinch-hitter, former Cardinal Dane Iorg. Without question this was a good per-centage decision. McRae was one of the best hitters in the American League, and Iorg had batted only .223 in limited use in 1985. But lo and behold, Iorg singled to right, and slow-footed catcher Sundberg eluded the tag of Darrell Porter to score the game-winning run. St. Louis had lost one of the most exciting games ever, 2–1. Ironically, it was the first time all season that the Cardinals had lost a game in the ninth inning.

Commentators compared the game to the stupendous sixth game of the 1975 World Series in which the Boston Red Sox defeated the Cincinnati Reds on a tense twelfth-inning homer off the bat of Carlton Fisk. The Royals-Cardinals contest in Game Six had, according to *Sports Illustrated* reporter Ron Fimrite, a "magical combination of excellence, luck, foolishness, irony, courage and gut-wrenching suspense that seems to find its way into this great sporting event year after year." While the game could not match the 1975 contest for sheer drama, as a standard in World Series play, few games could surpass it.

The Royals' win set up a dramatic seventh World Series game, something the Cardinals were not strangers to. But this time, they did not recover to take the championship. In fact, the game was an embarrassment as the Royals shut out the Cards 11–0. John Tudor started the big game, and the Cards had no better pitcher. He had already won two games in the series, and his Game Seven ap-pearance conjured up images of Bob Gibson winning three games in both 1964 and 1967. But Tudor fell behind early, while Bret Saberhagen sailed through the first few innings. The Cards did not even hit the ball out of the infield. When Tudor gave up five runs, Herzog pulled him, and the pitcher, although generally a genial person, proceeded to injure his hand by bashing a locker after leaving the game. Herzog went through two other pitchers, neither of whom could stop the Royals. Trailing 9–0 in the fifth, he inserted into the game his other pitching ace, Joaquin Andujar. The Royals continued their tear, and Andujar responded by putting on one of the ugliest displays ever witnessed in baseball. After home plate umpire Don Denkinger called an obvious ball on Jim Sundberg, Andujar flipped out. He stomped around the mound in what could only be called a temper tantrum and then charged toward Denkinger at the plate. Herzog rushed out to restrain Andujar and ended up arguing with Denkinger. In the end the umpire ejected Herzog from the game.

This made Herzog the first manager since bad boy Billy Martin of the Yankees in 1976 to get himself tossed out of a World Series game. Afterward, Herzog philosophized about this turn of events. "I'd seen enough," he said. "That wasn't a ball game. Like Casey says, 'Ain't no sense livin' in misery.' " He took the ejection as a reprieve from torture.

After Herzog left the field, Andujar returned to the mound, and on the very next pitch, called a ball by Denkinger, he flipped out again. He screamed and jumped up and down on the mound before running in to take a swing at Denkinger. By the time order had been restored, Andujar had been tossed out of the game as well. It was all over; the Royals added a couple of additional runs, but whatever hopes the Cardinals might have had for the seventh game were destroyed after Andujar's antics. One wit dubbed the Cardinals the "Nuthouse Gang." Ron Fimrite concluded, "The Cardinals were truly a sorry sight this night. Only a few days earlier they had seemed certain Series champions. Now they were exiting as buffoons."

In contrast, for the Royals a World Series victory proved exceedingly sweet after so many years of near misses. George Brett, who led the Royals attack with a .370 series average—just three percentage points ahead of Willie Wilson— summed up the victory with an insightful comment. As the bubbly flowed in the victory party following Game Seven, Brett shouted above the celebratory clamor taking place behind him, "I know, I know, people were saying, 'God, we've got this damn all-Missouri World Series. Who cares?' Well, do you think I wanted to be drafted by Kansas City, this little town in Missouri? I'm from L.A. and I wanted to play for the Dodgers. But I'll tell you something: I'm proud, very proud, to be a Kansas City Royal." Brett then laughed a big belly laugh and added, "And you know what it is we did, don't you? We showed 'em."

Never had Missouri enjoyed such fun! Never had its two greatest cities been so proud. Win or lose, both St. Louis and Kansas City had a wonderful time. And George Brett had been right, Missouri "showed 'em."

In retrospect, the two teams had been remarkably well matched. Both had strong defense, great pitching, and speed. The Royals' pitchers proved the difference between victory and defeat, however, as they successfully stopped the Cardinals' batters. St. Louis had a .185 team batting average for the series, and only Tito Landrum hit as high as .300. The Royals' pitchers compiled a 1.89 earned run average, led by Bret Saberhagen, who went 2–0 with a 0.50 ERA. No wonder they shut down the Cardinals' offense.

The world championship in 1985 proved to be the high-water mark of the Kansas City Royals. In the next fifteen seasons they failed to win even another division title. Much of the time they played .500 ball. The Cardinals had more success, winning the National League pennant in 1987, division titles in 1996 and 2000, and a wild-card playoff spot in 2001, but fell short of another World Series title. For an exciting few weeks in the fall of 1985, however, the two teams ruled the baseball world, and all eyes focused on Missouri. Those watching saw new heroes emerge to inspire young children and delight older fans. George Brett came to the fore as a likable star who did not want to play baseball anywhere except in his adopted home of Kansas City. Ozzie Smith of the Cardinals began to show the promise that Whitey Herzog had always believed was present. An unlikely pair of journeymen pitchers—Andujar and Tudor—showed what good pitchers could accomplish when backed up by outstanding defense, and a young fire-balling Bret Saberhagen emerged as a star in his own right. Collectively, the two Missouri teams continued to delight their fans long after the pivotal 1985 season.

Epilogue

Things Recent and (Con)Temporary

No Missouri baseball team has played in the World Series since 1987, when the Cardinals lost to the Minnesota Twins in a classic seven-game set. The Cardinals won division titles in 1996 and 2000 and also made the playoffs as a wild card team in 2001, but failed to advance to the fall classic. Enormous enthusiasm was generated during the summer of 1998 when Mark McGwire belted a record 70 home runs for St. Louis, besting Roger Maris's 61 round-trippers hit in 1961. The Royals, such a fine team during their first sixteen years of existence, descended into mediocrity after their championship season in 1985. From 1986 to 2000 the Royals failed to make it to the postseason, playing .484 ball and almost always finishing third or fourth in their division. The Cardinals did better, averaging .502 and usually finishing second or third.

The Last Stand of Whitey's Cardinals

In 1987, with almost the same personnel as the 1985 pennant-winning squad, the Cardinals returned to the World Series to face the Minnesota Twins of the American League. After the debacle of Game Seven in the 1985 World Series, Whitey Herzog decided to get rid of Joaquin Andujar, who had become as much of a "pill" as he was a talent for St. Louis. Herzog traded Andujar to the Oakland A's that winter, and thereafter Andujar's career wound down amidst injuries and accusations that an unspecified conspiracy prevented his continued success. Some of his injuries were legitimate, if inane. For instance, he hurt himself while taking batting practice, despite being in the American League, where pitchers do not bat because of the designated hitter rule.

With Jack Clark missing two-thirds of the season due to injury, the Cardinals slumped to 79–82 in 1986, a distant third in the National League East behind the New York Mets, who roared to the world championship over the Boston Red Sox. The Cards rebounded in 1987 to edge the Mets for the division championship as Clark (.286 average, 35 home runs, and 106 runs batted in) and outfielder Vince Coleman (.289 average and 109 stolen bases) enjoyed their finest seasons at the plate. Clark reinjured himself during the playoffs and made only a token appearance as the team edged San Francisco for the league championship. He missed the World Series altogether.

Ozzie Smith, who by this time had established himself as the greatest shortstop ever to play the position, had one of the most remarkable years ever in 1987. Not only his defense but also his offense was instrumental in the Cardinals' World Series run. Smith hit .303 with 43 stolen bases, 75 RBIs, and 104 runs scored and finished second in the Most Valuable Player Award balloting, behind the Cubs' Andre Dawson. Smith's performance, both at the plate and on the field, inspired an injury-riddled club to climb to the top of the National League East.

Whitey Herzog successfully managed first the Royals in the 1970s, then the Cardinals in the 1980s. Courtesy of the Kansas City Royals Baseball Club.

Prior to each of the Cardinals' three home games during the 1987 World Series, Smith put on a show with an awesome flurry of cartwheels, handsprings, and back flips. Thomas Boswell of the *Washington Post* wrote of him, "Instead of '1' his number should be '8,' but turned sideways because the possibilities he brings to his position are almost infinite."

In the 1987 National League Championship Series the Cardinals faced the San Francisco Giants, a bunch of free-swinging home-run hitters led by Will "The Thrill" Clark, Kevin Mitchell, Chili Davis, Mark Aldrete, Bob Brenly, and Jeffery Leonard. Against the Cardinals in the playoffs, Leonard batted .417 with five RBIs and a record-tying four homers. Rounding the bases with one arm immobile (one flap down) or both (two flaps down), Leonard created a stir en route to becoming the NLCS Most Valuable Player for that year. Despite the flaps, St. Louis winged its way to its third pennant in six years by shutting out the Giants over the final twenty-two innings. Catcher Tony Peña led the Cardinals' hitters with a .381 average in the playoffs, while the reliable John Tudor led the pitching staff with a 1.76 earned run average.

After dispatching the Giants in seven games, the Cardinals met the surprising Minnesota Twins in the World Series. The Twins were a hard-luck team that had never enjoyed much success. In a previous incarnation (as the Washington Senators between 1900 and 1960) the team had managed only three pennants—in 1924, 1925, and 1933—and one world championship. The decent teams of the 1920s and early 1930s were largely the result of the great Hall of Fame pitcher Walter Johnson, baseball's "Big Train," who dominated the American League for a generation. After escaping to Minneapolis for the 1961 season, the Twins brought an American League pennant to Minnesota in 1965, but lost in the World Series to the Los Angeles Dodgers and pitchers Sandy Koufax and Don Drysdale.

The Twins of the early 1980s were perhaps the poorest excuse for a baseball team that one could imagine. The 1982 squad lost a record 102 games. But something happened during that 1982 season that would change the team's fortunes and help rescue them from the depths of the American League. In April 1982 the Hubert H. Humphrey Metrodome opened in Minneapolis. The Twins' new ballpark soon gained the nickname "Homerdome" because of its short fences, lack of wind, and warm air that seemingly made balls jump out of the park. Enclosed by an inflatable roof—one wit suggested that it was like playing baseball inside a Hefty bag—the Metrodome also received the name "Thunderdome" because it was so effective in capturing high-decibel fan noise. This proved particularly distracting to visiting teams, and the Twins quickly exploited the advantage to become the best home-field team in the major leagues.

None of this meant much until August 1987, for beforehand the Twins were always mired at the bottom of the standings. But in 1987 the Twins began to impersonate a contender. They won a very tight American League West pennant race with a mediocre 85–77 record, but were 56–25, the league's best home record, in their "Hefty bag" stadium. They took the AL West in no small measure because of the poor play of the rest of its members; Kansas City finished second with an 83–79 record, and no one else in the division had a winning record. Few gave the Twins a chance in their playoff against the Detroit Tigers, winners of the East division with a major-league best 98–64 record, but the Twins took the series four games to one. The Twins, possessing the worst regular-season record of any pennant winner, were in the World Series.

This set up a remarkable contest with the Cardinals, in which for the first time in World Series history, the home team won every game. This was predictable, for the Twins had the third-worst road record in baseball in addition to the best home record. Minnesota swept the four games at the Metrodome amid waving "homer hankies" and off-the-charts decibel readings, and were swept in the three contests in St. Louis.

At the Metrodome, the Twins outscored the Cardinals 33–12. At Busch Stadium, their top four hitters combined for a .174 average with one homer. Series MVP Frank Viola went 2–1 with a 3.72 ERA and 16 strikeouts. Steve Lombardozzi batted .417, and Dan Gladden scored seven runs. With a .409 average, Tony Peña led the Cards, who played without Clark and got limited play from injured third baseman Terry Pendleton. For the series, the Twins out-homered the Cardinals seven to two and outscored them 38–25. So the Cardinals went home, defeated by a Twins team that had the worst record of any pennant winner. In the movie *Oh, God!* George Burns, playing God, says that the last miracle that He had performed was the victory of the New York Mets in the 1969 World Series. Of course, the movie was made in 1977, so it is entirely possible that God performed another miracle in 1987 by willing the victory of the Twins in the World Series. That is as good a way to explain the Cardinals' defeat as any.

Whitey Herzog's Cardinals never returned to postseason play. The team collapsed in 1988, finishing a dismal fifth in the division. St. Louis rebounded to third place in 1989, but then finished dead last in 1990 with a 70–92 record. It was the Cardinals' first last-place finish since 1918. On July 6, 1990, disgusted with the team's performance, Herzog resigned as manager. Red Schoendienst temporarily replaced him until Joe Torre was named manager on August 1. No one had enjoyed more success than Whitey Herzog in skippering the Cardinals, yet his inability to win either the 1985 or 1987 World Series colored the perceptions of many who commented on his leadership. As time passed Herzog seemed to have greater difficulty relating to the players, and clubhouse crises and conspiracies became increasingly common. Herzog had always taken the approach that he was in charge and everyone had better do as he said or suffer his wrath. Baseball analyst Bill James wrote quite perceptively that had Whitey Herzog not been a baseball manager he would probably have become a county sheriff. Herzog had gotten rid of such Cardinals greats as Keith Hernandez and Ted Simmons rather unceremoniously, but his style of management became less tolerated as times changed and the players asserted themselves more effectively during the era of free agency.

Herzog's replacement, Torre, had been one of the team's best players in the early 1970s, but his reign as Cardinals manager would simply be a stepping-stone before he moved on in the mid-1990s to a distinguished managing career with the New York Yankees. In addition to these changes, August A. Busch died, bringing to an end nearly forty years of paternalistic ownership.

The Poignant Story of the Royals' Dick Howser

The manager of the 1985 World Champion Royals, Dick Howser, had been a modest, thoughtful, and easygoing player with the hapless Kansas City Athletics and Cleveland Indians in the 1960s. Between 1981 and 1986 he guided Kansas City to a remarkable 507–425 record, a .544 winning percentage. But two days after he managed the American League to an All-Star game victory in 1986, doctors diagnosed him with a brain tumor. Howser left the team almost immediately and underwent surgery. It appeared that all would be well.

While he did not rejoin the Royals for the rest of the 1986 season, on October 10 the team announced that Howser would return to manage the club the next season. But by spring Howser had not recovered. On February 23, 1987, just three days after the Royals' spring training camp opened, he abandoned his attempt to come back and gave up his position as manager. Billy Gardner was named as his successor. A pall hung over the Royals that whole season. They played poorly, to be sure, and many thought they were distracted by Howser's situation. On June 17 Dick Howser passed away in Kansas City. The Royals retired his uniform number, 10, in a moving ceremony at Royals Stadium on July 3.

It is hard to determine how much the death of Howser affected the play of the Royals. He had been exceptionally likable and exceedingly effective as a leader. Reporter Steve Cameron appropriately concluded in his history of the team, "Firings and clubhouse squabbles are one thing, but the Howser tragedy tore at the heart of the Royals—from the top on down, from owner to bat-boys, pitchers to secretaries. Dick Howser's death rocked Kansas City, too, washing the

Dick Howser, Kansas City Royals manager. Courtesy of the Kansas City Royals Baseball Club.

community with a sense of loss and the feeling of being left without its baseball rudder. The man seemed to stand for everything the franchise believed, everything it had worked to achieve, and suddenly he was gone."

In addition to the emotional void left by Howser's passing, the Royals had no one who could fill his shoes on the field. The team went through a succession of managers, including two of the team's great former players, John Wathan and Hal McRae. Wathan guided the Royals to their best showing in the post-1985 period, a second-place finish with a 90–72 record in 1989. But after a pair of sixth-place finishes in 1990 and 1991 he was replaced by McRae. For his part, McRae was only able to motivate the team to third place in 1993 and 1994, and then he was gone as well. Managers Bob Boone and Tony Muser also failed to lead the Royals to the kind of success enjoyed under Howser, and before him Jim Frey and Whitey Herzog. The Royals have consistently finished with losing records since 1995.

Perhaps the most significant year for the Royals in the 1990s was 1993. That is when George Brett played the twenty-first and final season of his illustrious career. Brett was a surefire bet to reach the Hall of Fame in his first year of eligibility, and in 1999 he was inducted. Equally important, Ewing Kauffman, the club's founder and owner, died in August 1993, bequeathing the team to his wife, Muriel, but making plans in his will for its eventual transfer to the Kansas City community. Within days of his death the stadium was renamed Kauffman Stadium in his honor.

Bo Knows Baseball

After winning the Heisman Trophy as the greatest college football player in 1985, Auburn University's Bo Jackson was persuaded by the Royals to sign with them instead of with the Tampa Bay Buccaneers in the National Football League. Jackson joined the Royals after just fifty-three games in the minors. While showing speed and power, he struck out frequently and too often displayed questionable defense. In his first major-league at bat on September 2, 1986, Jackson hit a monstrous home run that many took as a portent of his great ability. Could Bo Jackson be the next-generation Hall of Famer for the Royals, someone who would pick up the mantle of George Brett? Many people thought so at the time.

Kansas City Monarchs star Buck O'Neil described in his autobiography how he heard a unique crack from Bo Jackson's bat, a sound he had heard only three times in his life. He wrote that he first heard it from Babe Ruth. "It wasn't so much the *sight* of him that got to me as the *sound*," O'Neil wrote. "When Ruth was hitting the ball, it was a distinct sound, like a small stick of dynamite going off." That sound set Ruth apart from everyone else. "The next time I heard that sound was in 1938, my first year with the Monarchs. We were in Griffith Stadium in Washington to play the Homestead Grays, and I heard that sound all the way up in the clubhouse, so I ran down to the dugout in just my pants and my sweatshirt to see who was hitting the ball. And it was Josh Gibson. I thought, my land, that's a powerful man."

O'Neil then added, "I didn't hear it again for almost fifty years. I thought I'd never hear it again. But I was at Royals Stadium, scouting the American League for the Cubs, and I came out of the press room and was going down to field level when I heard that ball sound as if the Babe or Josh were still down there. Pow! Pow! Pow! It was Bo Jackson—the Royals had just called him up." O'Neil certainly understood baseball, and he was convinced that Jackson had the talent to become one of the greatest players ever.

Jackson was also a media celebrity from the very beginning. Steve Cameron observed, "Bo was a one-man circus. He drew crowds like Elvis or Princess Di . . . Bo was the Royals' biggest attraction ever. Never mind that Brett, a future Hall of Famer, shared the same dugout, George was ignored like a utility infielder whenever the Bo Show came to town." That star power caused jealousy in the clubhouse and a certain amount of tension within the Royals' organization, but as long as Jackson performed on the field any complaints sounded hollow. In 1987, Jackson's first full season in a Royals uniform, he batted only .235, but he also hit 22 home runs. While his average could stand improvement, the homers were welcome.

Jackson announced late in 1987 that he intended to play professional football with the Los Angeles Raiders as a "hobby" in the off-season. His teammates immediately criticized him for not taking baseball seriously enough, a criticism that was both accurate and beside the point. While he did not make baseball his life, like his teammates did, Jackson also had such enormous talent that he could pursue other sports and perform well in everything he did. Unfortunately, had he decided to commit himself only to baseball he would probably still be playing and headed to Cooperstown at the end of a long and illustrious career. Jackson responded poorly to these criticisms and found himself at the center of a controversy in Kansas City, as many questioned if he would ever fit in there. He found himself booed on the field and castigated in the media. Many Kansas City fans were displeased that Jackson would play for the Raiders, the loathed arch-rivals of their city's football team, the Chiefs. For them, seeing Bo come to town dressed in Raiders' silver and black was a sacrilege, akin to seeing Brett in Yankee pinstripes. In some respects, Bo Jackson was more suited to the spotlights of New York or Los Angeles than to the traditional culture of Kansas City.

Even so, every year that he played for the Royals, Jackson's performance improved. In 1988 he slammed 25 homers and stole 27 bases, but still struck out 146 times. However, in 1989 he finally raised his batting average to .256, hit 32 home runs with 105 RBIs, and used his speed and strong arm to become one of the most exciting left fielders in baseball. That year he made the All-Star squad for his first and only time. In his last year in Kansas City in 1990, Jackson raised his average to .272, while still hitting 28 homers.

Jackson suffered a serious hip injury while playing for the Raiders in the 1990–1991 football season. The Royals fully believed he was finished because of this injury and gave him an unconditional release at the beginning of the 1991 baseball season. Jackson then signed with the Chicago White Sox, but played only twenty-three games before realizing he could not continue. He received enormous sympathy for his attempt to come back, but it was painful just watching him try to run bases and chase fly balls. Such an elegant player previously, he appeared as but a shadow of the athlete who had performed so well for the Royals. Jackson submitted to a hip replacement and tried to come back in 1993. He saw part-time service as a designated hitter with the White Sox in 1993 and the California Angels in 1994 but never performed as he had with the Royals.

Bo Jackson took the American League by storm in the late 1980s.
Courtesy of the Kansas City Royals Baseball Club.

It was a sad end to the career of Bo Jackson. Some would say it was a tragedy, and they would not be far off. Of the three sluggers that Buck O'Neil wrote about, all might be considered tragic figures. Babe Ruth, of course, had an enormously successful career in the major leagues, but that success was never equaled in the other areas of his life, and he died earlier than the normal three score and ten years with his last years riddled by despair. Josh Gibson, the "black Babe Ruth," hit more home runs in the Negro Leagues than anyone else but never got a chance to play in the major leagues. He suffered a brain tumor in 1945 just as the National League was on the verge of being integrated, and we will never know how good he might have been in the majors. Bo Jackson had his shot in baseball and showed flashes of excellence, but his career was cut short by an injury that took place on a football field. Had both Josh Gibson and Bo Jackson been able to play a full career in the major leagues they probably would have been among the greatest in the game. Buck O'Neil was right: all three had unique gifts.

Tony LaRussa and the 1996 Cardinals

Aside from some remarkable individual performances, such as reliever Lee Smith's record forty-seven saves in 1991, the St. Louis Cardinals had only modest success in the early 1990s. The Cardinals finished second in 1991 and third in 1992 and 1993, but then weak hitting dropped them to below .500 in 1994, as they played for the first time in the National League's new Central Division.

Because of this performance, in 1995 the Cards sacked Joe Torre and brought in former A's pilot Tony LaRussa for the 1996 season.

The Cardinals won their first National League Central Division title in 1996, with an 88–74 record, after winning only 62 games the year before. Then they dispatched the San Diego Padres in three games in the divisional playoffs. This set up a seven-game National League Championship Series with the Atlanta Braves, the winningest team of the 1990s and the defending world champions. After losing the first game, 4–2, the Cardinals came back to take the next three in the series. At that point, everyone was talking about the Cardinals returning to the World Series for the first time since 1987. After all, no team in the NLCS had ever rallied from a 3–1 deficit to advance to the World Series. "Somebody's got to do it," Braves third baseman Chipper Jones said. "Might as well be us." Unfortunately for the Cardinals, it was. Only seven teams had overcome such a deficit in postseason history. And only one team had twice lost 3–1 leads—St. Louis. Atlanta stood one loss from elimination when Cardinals' catcher Tom Pagnozzi commented, "If there's one team that can win three in a row, it's Atlanta. They have three Cy Young Award winners all lined up."

The last three games were embarrassments for the Cardinals. They were outscored 32–1; they lost 14–0 in Game Five and 15–0 in Game Seven. The Braves' three ace starters, John Smoltz, Greg Maddux, and Tom Glavine, cruised. The Cardinals' defeat put the Braves in their fourth World Series in six years, where they lost to Joe Torre's New York Yankees.

Post mortem on this defeat has revolved largely around the role of Tony LaRussa as a manager. He had enjoyed enormous success in Oakland, managing three pennant winners in 1988, 1989, and 1990. But he was able to bring the world championship to Oakland only in 1989, during the "earthquake" series with the San Francisco Giants, even though the 1988 and 1990 teams were arguably much more accomplished. The reason, many people believe, was the tightness with which LaRussa was wound. His teams felt intense pressure from him to perform, and a choke too often took place in the big games. The Cardinals had everything going for them through the first four games of the NLCS in 1996 and should have been able to win one of the last three. Could pressure emanating from LaRussa have played a role in the classic choke of 1996? Perhaps, but it is also possible that had LaRussa not been in place the Cardinals would not have even reached the playoffs.

Big news came after the season. In December 1996 Anheuser-Busch sold the Cardinals for $150 million to an investment group headed by St. Louis banker Andrew Baur and William DeWitt, Jr., whose father had once owned the Browns and the Reds.

The Home Run Comes to St. Louis

For thirty years everyone believed that no one would ever consistently hit home runs in spacious Busch Memorial Stadium. Whitey Herzog elevated that belief into an article of faith and built championship teams on speed rather than power. And, indeed, no one regularly put up big home run totals in St. Louis— until 1997. In midseason of that year the Cardinals acquired Mark McGwire, better known as "Big Mac," in a trade with the Oakland A's. McGwire was playing out the last year of his contract and made it known to everyone that he wanted to leave Oakland. Tony LaRussa, who had managed McGwire with the A's, persuaded the Cardinals' front office to trade for the power-hitting first baseman. LaRussa was convinced that once McGwire arrived in St. Louis, he would see what a wonderful city it was and what terrific fans the Cardinals had, and he would want to stay. Even if he chose to move on at the end of the 1997 season, LaRussa reasoned, McGwire might be the offensive punch required to return to the playoffs that year and not be humiliated the way the Cards had been in Games Five and Seven the previous fall. LaRussa's instincts proved correct, and late in the season McGwire signed with St. Louis instead of opting for free agency. McGwire hit 58 home runs in 1997, becoming the only player other than Babe Ruth to hit 50 or more home runs in consecutive seasons. But McGwire would soon make even more history.

In 1998, Mark McGwire broke the single-season home run record by hitting 70 home runs. It was a magical, momentous event for all of baseball and especially for the St. Louis Cardinals. The 1998 season started auspiciously enough. On opening day in St. Louis on March 31, 1998, McGwire hit a grand slam to start the chase for the record. Pundits observed that with this "dinger" he was on a pace to hit 162 for the season. Within the first week he hit four homers, and the race was on. Several other sluggers also got off to a fast start, Ken Griffey, Jr., and Alex Rodriguez of the Seattle Mariners and Andres Gallaraga of the Atlanta Braves among them. None could quite catch McGwire, however, as he set a sizzling home run pace through the first half of the season. This competition inspired everyone. It inspired the hitters as they vied for the home run title, and perhaps the single-season record. It inspired the fans, who had not seen such excitement for years and were naturally jaded by the periodic labor disputes in the sport. It inspired the sports media, who gave it far more attention than even the best pennant races had enjoyed in previous years. It inspired even the larger public that normally was indifferent to baseball. Ultimately, it inspired the world, as Europeans, who lived for soccer rather than baseball, enthusiastically followed the race for the home run title.

By the time of the All-Star break it had become obvious that the National League home run title would go to either McGwire or Sammy Sosa of the Chicago Cubs. Sosa had come out of nowhere in June and early July to challenge McGwire's home run lead. On July 28 McGwire had 45 homers to Sosa's 41. But Sammy closed the gap and on August 11 it was McGwire with 47 and Sosa with 45. At a highly touted Cardinals-Cubs match-up on August 19 at Wrigley Field the fans were not disappointed. Sosa slammed his 48th home run in the fifth inning to go past McGwire for the first time all season. But in the eighth McGwire parked his 48th homer in the bleachers to tie the game, then won the game in the tenth with his 49th homer of the season.

In part the competition between McGwire and Sosa was part and parcel of a long-standing rivalry between the Cardinals and Cubs. They had played in the same division for decades and often fought it out on the field. McGwire was a big, strapping, attractive white man. Sosa, from the Dominican Republic, was an equally attractive black man. One of the wonderful things about the home run championship was that it would not be decided by anything but how well the two men hit against the same pitchers throughout the season. Perhaps the best thing was how the two players related to each other. Sosa was an extrovert who seemingly loved the spotlight and never disappointed when called upon to meet the public. He had a little hand gesture that alternated between his heart and his head that everyone enjoyed. Kids throughout the nation were doing that gesture of goodwill throughout the summer. McGwire was naturally more introverted and did not enjoy the spotlight in the same way, but rose to the occasion and did not disappoint his adoring fans. These two men met each other on the field and talked when one was on first base and the other playing the field, and when they were warming up before the game. It was clear that they respected each other. Their friendly rivalry showed, and it made everyone feel good. People began to think that perhaps baseball was about not only money and power, but also enjoying an afternoon or evening outside at a childhood game with a long tradition. Perhaps it was more about what took place on the field than off.

The camaraderie and joy in the experience of 1998 was present for all to see. Both players said they would not be disappointed regardless of who won the home run title. "What Sammy and I have done, whoever is on top, nobody should be disappointed," McGwire said. "How can you walk away disappointed? You can't. It's impossible." Both carried the summer with joy and grace and dignity.

McGwire and Sosa conjured a true sense of nostalgia during the 1998 season, even as they raced to set a new home run record. Perhaps, best of all, both did set a new record. When the season ended McGwire had 70 home runs, besting Roger Maris's single-season record of 61. But Sosa passed Maris as well, hitting 66. When asked if he was disappointed at having finished second in the race, Sosa said at season's end, "Disappointed for what? I didn't think for any moment I would get disappointed. I'm happy for Mark. I'm happy for myself. Mark is my friend." Between them, McGwire and Sosa set an entirely new standard of excellence. In 1999 they again both topped 60 home runs, making them the only players in history to hit more than 60 in two different seasons. McGwire hit his 500th career home run in 1999 as well.

The Cardinals Return to the Postseason, 2000–2001

The Cards started the 2000 season with a bang, acquiring American League Gold Glove center fielder Jim Edmonds right before the beginning of the season. This acquisition along with improved pitching helped solidify the team and allowed it to compete for the Central Division championship. In the middle of the season, Mark McGwire was injured and looked to be out for most of the season. This event helped spawn another memorable moment, when the St. Louis Cardinals acquired Will Clark from the Baltimore Orioles. Clark helped propel the Cardinals to the playoffs, as the team ended up ten games ahead of the second-place Cincinnati Reds. The Cardinals then swept the Atlanta Braves in a best-of-five series to face the New York Mets for the National League title. Unfortunately, the Mets defeated the Cards in five games. LaRussa's Cardinals failed to reach the World Series for the second time, after coming close.

In October 2000 Will Clark retired from baseball, saying that he had done everything he had wanted to do and wished to go out on top. He did so by retiring as a member of the St. Louis Cardinals, a team he had always admired as one of the best in the National League. On November 7, 2000, two Cardinals were honored with Gold Glove Awards: Edmonds, and catcher Mike Matheny.

In 2001 the Cards turned around what started as a mediocre season, coming on strong after the All-Star break to finish as co-champions of the Central Division. With a 40–18 record in the last two months of the season, they climbed over the Cubs and finally tied the Astros with a season record of 93–69. In the process the Cardinals notched an excellent paid attendance of 3,020,046 for the year. In the playoffs they met the Arizona Diamondbacks, an expansion team created in 1997 that featured the pitching of twenty-game winners Randy Johnson and Curt Schilling. Riding their stunning pitching performances, the Diamondbacks defeated the Cardinals and went on to win the world championship. The Cards pushed Arizona to a winner-take-all fifth game, which they lost in the bottom of the ninth inning. It was a disappointing end to an exciting season, highlighted by an outstanding performance from rookie Albert Pujols. The twenty-one-year-old hit .329 with 37 home runs and 130 RBIs, becoming the first rookie to lead St. Louis in all three Triple Crown categories since Rogers Hornsby in 1916 and the first Cardinal of any experience level to do so since Ted Simmons in 1973. Although born in the Dominican Republic, Pujols was something of a native Missourian, having moved with his father at age sixteen to the Midwest and attended high school in Independence, Missouri. Then he spent a year at Maple Woods Junior College in Kansas City before being selected by the Cardinals in the thirteenth round of the 1999 draft. After the 2001 season, Pujols was named the National League's Rookie of the Year, the first Cardinal to win the award since Todd Worrell in 1986. It was the beginning of what many expect to be a superlative career.

Equally significant, future Hall of Famer Mark McGwire announced after the season that he was ending his exceptional sixteen-year major-league career. The first baseman, whose single-season home run record was broken in 2001 by San Francisco's Barry Bonds, retired with 583 career homers, fifth on the all-time list. McGwire told the media that he was "worn out" and had decided not to sign the two-year, $30 million contract extension the Cardinals had offered. "After a considerable discussion with those close to me, I have decided not to sign the extension, as I am unable to perform at a level equal to the salary the organization would be paying me," McGwire said in a rather classy statement. "I believe I owe it to the Cardinals and the fans of St. Louis to step aside, so a talented free agent can be brought in as the final piece of what I expect can be a world-championship-caliber team."

McGwire had missed the second half of the 2000 season because of a sore right knee and underwent surgery to correct patella tendinitis in October of that year. Although it typically takes twelve months to come back from that procedure, McGwire was in the 2001 opening-day lineup. But not long thereafter his knee began giving him problems again, and for the season he hit a career-low .187 with 29 homers in 97 games. McGwire's efforts in the playoffs were painful to watch as he had just one hit in eleven at bats, with six strikeouts, against the Diamondbacks. Still, McGwire is certain to join two other great players who retired in 2001, Tony Gwynn of the San Diego Padres and Cal Ripken of the Baltimore Orioles, at induction ceremonies for the National Baseball Hall of Fame in 2007.

Conclusion

In the twenty-first century the fortunes of the Cardinals and Royals may be strikingly different from what has gone before. They may also be a continuation of both past successes and failures. An independent review sponsored by Major League Baseball in July 2000 pointed to serious structural problems with the game that portend doom for small-market teams such as the Royals and the Cardinals. It found that despite impressive industry-wide revenue growth in the 1990s, Major League Baseball "has an outdated economic structure that has created an unacceptable level of revenue disparity and competitive imbalance over the same period. The growing gap between the 'have' and the 'have not' clubs—which is to say the minority that have a realistic chance of succeeding in post-season play and the majority of clubs that have poor prospects of reaching the postseason—is a serious and imminent threat to the popularity, health, stability and growth of the game."

The study went on to conclude, "In recent years, there has been a rapidly accelerating disparity in revenues and, consequently, payrolls between clubs in high- and low-revenue markets. There also has been a stronger correlation between club revenues/payrolls and on-field competitiveness." The report's authors sounded the alarm that unless these disparities are addressed, the game will become one in which only large-market teams will be able to win championships.

As evidence of this, one can point to the fact that the New York Yankees appeared in five of six World Series between 1996 and 2001, winning four of them. Of course, one could make the case that small-market teams have always had an uphill battle in achieving success on the playing field—after all, New York, Los Angeles, and Chicago teams have won the World Series forty-one times since the inauguration of the fall classic in 1903—but there have been notable dynasties created by the Cardinals, Reds, A's, Royals, Braves, Indians, and Pirates without benefit of big money available from major media outlets. One could hope that will continue in the new century.

Excellent front-office management, not exceptional cash flow, brought the Cardinals and the Royals their successes. The Yankees and Mets, the Dodgers and Angels, and the Cubs and White Sox will always have more money to invest than other teams because of the market size they serve. But those are not guarantors of success. Indeed, the Angels, Cubs, and White Sox have demonstrated absolutely no ability since 1945 to win championships, and the Dodgers and Mets have enjoyed only intermittent and mixed success. The Yankees stand alone as the team with the greatest capability to transform its cash flow into championship teams. Perhaps, Major League Baseball should simply do away with that partic- ular franchise, disbursing its players elsewhere and replacing it with an entirely new expansion team. Would that help small-market teams achieve parity?

That suggestion has about as much chance of achieving success as several of the recommendations offered by the blue ribbon panel. The review commission wanted to institute the following recommendations:

1. Revenue sharing to at least 40 percent of all member clubs' local revenue;
2. For competitive balance, a 50 percent tax on club payrolls that are above a fixed threshold of $84 million, with all clubs encouraged to have a minimum payroll of $40 million;
3. Central fund distributions to be made by the Commissioner to improve competitive balance, creating a "Commissioner's Pool" that is allocated to assist low-revenue clubs in improving their competitiveness and in meeting the minimum payroll obligation of $40 million;
4. A competitive balance draft in which the weakest eight clubs would have a unique opportunity to select players in the organizations, but not on the forty-man rosters, of the eight clubs that qualified for the playoffs;
5. Implementing reforms in the Rule 4 draft;
6. Allowing strategic franchise relocations to address the competitive issues facing the game. Clubs that have little likelihood of securing a new ballpark or undertaking other revenue-enhancing activities should have the option of relocation if better markets can be identified.

Of these six recommendations, only the last two have much chance of gaining approval. Revenue sharing has been discussed for decades, but the owners in the large-market cities have never wanted to see it implemented. They will continue to oppose it, and there does not seem to be any way out of that morass. The same holds true for a competitive balance tax. The commissioner's pool also has the same problem. All of these are a form of welfare for the weaker teams, and successful owners have the same perspective on welfare that successful business people have on it for the larger society—let those people go out, work hard, and achieve success just like me. If they cannot make it in the marketplace then perhaps they are not savvy enough to succeed. In relation to the fourth recommendation, clubs that make the playoffs are doing something right, and they will be unwilling to let the worst teams in baseball take away their players, probably their younger players who are being groomed for future greatness by playing a few seasons in the minor leagues.

It is doubtful that either the Cardinals or the Royals or any other small-market team will receive any assistance from these proposed changes to the business of baseball. Of course they may not need it. The Cardinals remain one of the best teams in the National League and have division titles to prove it. The Royals seem to be making good strides in rebuilding after wandering in the wilderness for the last fifteen years. However these teams progress in the new century, they will bring an excitement to the state of Missouri. Missourians have enjoyed a love affair with baseball for more than a century, and that will not end anytime soon. Both Kansas City and St. Louis remain popular baseball towns where players like to work and fans love their teams. That may ultimately be the greatest constant of major-league baseball in Missouri.

Selected Bibliography

General Histories

Abrams, Roger I. *Legal Bases: Baseball and the Law.* Philadelphia: Temple University Press, 1998.

Alexander, Charles C. *Our Game: An American Baseball History.* New York: Henry Holt, 1991.

Betts, John R. "The Technological Revolution and the Rise of Sports, 1850–1880." *Mississippi Valley Historical Review* 40 (1953): 231–56.

Bjarkman, Peter C. *Encyclopedia of Major League Baseball: American League.* New York: Carroll and Graf, 1991.

Boswell, Thomas. *Why Time Begins on Opening Day.* Garden City, N.Y.: Doubleday and Co., 1984.

Burk, Robert F. *Never Just a Game: Players, Owners, and American Baseball to 1920.* Chapel Hill: University of North Carolina Press, 1994.

Chalmers, David Mark. *And the Crooked Places Made Straight: The Struggle for Social Change in the 1960s.* Baltimore: Johns Hopkins University Press, 1996.

Chandler, Happy. *Heroes, Plain Folks, and Skunks: The Life and Times of Happy Chandler.* Chicago: Bonus Books, 1989.

Craig, Peter S. "Monopsony in Manpower: Organized Baseball Meets Antitrust Laws." *Yale Law Review* 60 (March 1953): 576–639.

Crepeau, Richard C. *Baseball: America's Diamond Mind, 1918–1941.* Orlando: University of Central Florida Press, 1980.

Dewey, Donald, and Nicholas Acocella. *The Biographical History of Baseball.* New York: Carroll and Graf, 1995.

Dickinson, Dan, and Kieran Dickinson. *Major League Stadiums: A Vacation Planning Reference to the 26 Baseball Parks.* Jefferson, N.C.: McFarland and Co., 1991.

Falkner, David. *Nine Sides of the Diamond: Baseball's Great Glove Men on the Fine Art of Defense.* New York: Times Books, 1990.

Freedman, Stephen. "The Baseball Fad in Chicago, 1865–1870: An Exploration of the Role of Sport in the Nineteenth-Century City." *Journal of Sport History* 5 (summer 1978): 43–53.

Funk, Daniel Carl. "Fan Loyalty: The Structure and Stability of an Individual's Loyalty toward an Athletic Team." Ph.D. diss., Ohio State University, 1998.

Goldstein, Richard. *Spartan Seasons: How Baseball Survived the Second World War.* New York: Macmillan, 1980.

Goldstein, Warren. *Playing for Keeps: A History of Early Baseball.* Ithaca, N.Y.: Cornell University Press, 1989.

Helyar, John. *Lords of the Realm: The Real History of Baseball.* New York: Villard Books, 1994.

James, Bill. *The Bill James Guide to Baseball Managers from 1870 to Today.* New York: Scribner, 1997.

Kirsch, George B. *The Creation of American Team Sports: Baseball and Cricket, 1838–72.* Urbana: University of Illinois Press, 1989.

Koppett, Leonard. *Koppett's Concise History of Major League Baseball.* Philadelphia: Temple University Press, 1998.

———. *The Man in the Dugout: Baseball's Top Managers and How They Got That Way.* New York: Crown Publishers, 1993.

Kuhn, Bowie. *Hard Ball: The Education of a Baseball Commissioner.* New York: Times Books, 1987.

LaBlanc, Michael L., ed. *Professional Sports Team Histories: Baseball.* Detroit: Gale Research, Inc., 1994.

Lansche, Jerry. *Glory Fades Away: The Nineteenth Century World Series Rediscovered.* Dallas: Taylor Publishing Co., 1991.

Lowery, Phillip J. *Green Cathedrals: The Ultimate Celebration of all 271 Major League and Negro League Ballparks, Past and Present.* Reading, Mass.: Addison-Wesley Publishing Co., 1992.

Miller, Marvin. *A Whole Different Ballgame: The Sport and Business of Baseball.* New York: Carol Publishing Group, 1991.

Mrozek, Donald. *Sport and American Mentality, 1880–1910.* Knoxville: University of Tennessee Press, 1983.

Murdock, Eugene C. *Ban Johnson: Czar of Baseball.* Westport, Conn.: Greenwood Press, 1982.

Neal-Lunsford, Jeff. "Sport in the Land of Television: The Use of Sport in Network Prime-Time Schedules, 1946–50." *Journal of Sport History* 19 (spring 1992): 56–76.

Rader, Benjamin G. *Baseball: A History of America's Game.* Urbana: University of Illinois Press, 1992.

Riess, Steven A. *City Games: The Evolution of American Urban Society and the Rise of Sports.* Urbana: University of Illinois Press, 1989.

————. *Touching Base: Professional Baseball and American Culture in the Progressive Era.* Rev. ed. Urbana: University of Illinois Press, 1999.

Ritter, Lawrence S. *The Glory of Their Times: The Story of the Early Days of Baseball Told by the Men Who Played It.* New York: Vintage Books, 1985.

Scully, Gerald W. *The Business of Major League Baseball.* Chicago: University of Chicago Press, 1989.

Seymour, Harold. *Baseball: The Early Years.* New York: Oxford University Press, 1960.

————. *Baseball: The Golden Age.* New York: Oxford University Press, 1971.

Shatzin, Mike, ed. *The Ballplayers: Baseball's Ultimate Biographical Reference.* New York: William Morrow and Co., 1990.

Skolnik, Richard. *Baseball and the Pursuit of Innocence: A Fresh Look at the Old Ball Game.* College Station: Texas A&M University Press, 1994.

Spaulding, Albert G. *America's National Game.* St. Louis: American Sports Publishing Co., 1911.

Sullivan, Dean A. "Faces in the Crowd: A Statistical Portrait of Baseball Spectators in Cincinnati, 1886–1888." *Journal of Sport History* 17 (winter 1990): 353–65.

Thorn, John, and Pete Palmer, with Michael Gershman, eds. *Total Baseball.* 4th ed. New York: Viking, 1995.

Turner, Frederick. *When the Boys Came Back: Baseball and 1946.* New York: Henry Holt and Co., 1996.

Voigt, David Quentin. *American Baseball.* 3 vols. Norman: University of Oklahoma Press, 1966–1970.

Ward, Geoffrey, with Ken Burns. *Baseball: An Illustrated History.* New York: Alfred A. Knopf, 1994.

White, G. Edward. *Creating the National Pastime: Baseball Transforms Itself, 1903–1953.* Princeton, N.J.: Princeton University Press, 1996.

The Negro Leagues

Clark, Dick, and Larry Lester, eds. *The Negro Leagues Book.* Cleveland: Society for American Baseball Research, 1994.

Lamb, Chris, and Glen Bleske. "Democracy on the Field: The Black Press Takes on White Baseball." *Journalism History* 24 (summer 1998): 51–59.

Levy, Scott Jarman. "Tricky Ball: 'Cool Papa' Bell and Life in the Negro Leagues." *Gateway Heritage* 9 (spring 1989): 26–35.

Peterson, Robert. *Only the Ball Was White: A History of Black Players and All-Black Professional Teams.* New York: Random House, 1970.

Riley, James A. *The Biographical Encyclopedia of the Negro Baseball Leagues.* New York: Carroll and Graf, 1994.

Rogosin, Donn. *Invisible Men: Life in Baseball's Negro Leagues.* New York: Atheneum, 1983.

Sammons, Jeffrey T. " 'Race' and Sport: A Critical, Historical Examination." *Journal of Sport History* 21 (fall 1994): 203–78.

Simons, William. "Jackie Robinson and the American Mind: Journalistic Perceptions of the Reintegration of Baseball." *Journal of Sport History* 12 (spring 1985): 39–64.

Tygiel, Jules. *Baseball's Great Experiment: Jackie Robinson and His Legacy.* New York: Oxford University Press, 1983.

Wiggins, David K. "Wendell Smith, the *Pittsburgh Courier-Journal* and the Campaign to Include Blacks in Organized Baseball, 1933–1945." *Journal of Sport History* 10 (summer 1983): 5–29.

Young, A. S. *Great Negro Baseball Stars, and How They Made the Major Leagues.* New York: A. S. Barnes, 1953.

Missouri Baseball

Broeg, Bob. *The One Hundred Greatest Moments in St. Louis Sports.* St. Louis: Missouri Historical Society Press, 2000.

———. *Bob Broeg: Memories of a Hall of Fame Sportswriter.* Champaign, Ill.: Sagamore Publishing, 1995.

Carter, Gregg Lee. "Baseball in St. Louis, 1867–1875: An Historical Case Study in Civic Pride." *Missouri Historical Society Bulletin* 31 (July 1975): 253–63.

Cash, Jon David. "The Spirit of St. Louis in the History of Major League Baseball, 1875–1891." Ph.D. diss., University of Oregon, 1995.

Clevenger, Martha R. "St. Louis's Barometer." *Gateway Heritage* 10 (winter 1989): 46–49.

Lampe, Anthony B. "The Background of Professional Baseball in St. Louis." *Missouri Historical Society Bulletin* 7 (October 1950): 6–34.

Mormino, Gary. "The Playing Fields of St. Louis: Italian Immigrants and Sport, 1925–1941." *Journal of Sport History* 9 (summer 1982): 5–16.

Seymour, Harold. "St. Louis and the Union Baseball War." *Missouri Historical Review* 51 (April 1957): 257–69.

Kansas City Athletics

Bird, Stephen V. "Ernest Mehl: A Sports Editor's Role in a City's Acquisition of Two Major League Franchises." Master's thesis, Central Missouri State University, 1992.

Boudreau, Lou, with Russell Schneider. *Covering All the Bases*. Champaign, Ill.: Sagamore Publishing, 1993.

Clark, Tom. *Champagne and Baloney: A History of Finley's A's*. New York: Harper and Row, 1976.

Duplacey, James, and Joséph Romain. *Baseball's Great Dynasties: The Athletics*. New York: Gallery Books, 1991.

Kuklick, Bruce. "The Demise of the Philadelphia Athletics." *Baseball History* 3 (1990): 33–48.

———. *To Every Thing a Season: Shibe Park and Urban Philadelphia, 1909–1976*. Princeton, N.J.: Princeton University Press, 1991.

Libby, Bill. *Charlie O. and the Angry A's*. Garden City, N.Y.: Doubleday and Co., 1975.

Macht, Norman L. "Philadelphia Athletics—Kansas City Athletics—Oakland A's: Three Families and Three Baseball Epochs." In Peter C. Bjarkman, ed., *Encyclopedia of Major League Baseball: American League Team Histories*. Rev. ed. New York: Carroll and Graf Publishers, 1993, 293–357.

Mehl, Ernest. *The Kansas City Athletics*. New York: Henry Holt, 1956.

Michelson, Herbert. *Charlie O.: Charles Oscar Finley vs. the Baseball Establishment*. Indianapolis: Bobbs-Merrill, 1973.

Kansas City Monarchs

Bruce, Janet. *The Kansas City Monarchs: Champions of Black Baseball*. Lawrence: University Press of Kansas, 1985.

Holway, John B. *Josh and Satch: The Life and Times of Josh Gibson and Satchel Paige*. New York: Carroll and Graf Publishers/Richard Gallen, 1991.

O'Neil, Buck, and Steve Wulf. *I Was Right on Time: My Journey from the Negro Leagues to the Majors*. New York: Fireside Books, 1997.

Paige, Leroy. *Maybe I'll Pitch Forever*. Garden City, N.Y.: Doubleday and Co., 1962.

———. *Pitchin' Man*. N.p., 1948.

Ribowsky, Mark. *Don't Look Back: Satchel Paige in the Shadows of Baseball*. New York: Da Capo Press, 1994.

Trouppe, Quincy. *20 Years Too Soon: Prelude to Major-League Integrated Baseball*. St. Louis: Missouri Historical Society Press, 1995.

Kansas City Royals

Bordman, Sid. *Expansion to Excellence: An Intimate Portrait of the Kansas City Royals.* Marceline, Mo.: Walsworth Publishing Co., 1981.

Brett, George, with Steve Cameron. *George Brett: From Here to Cooperstown.* Lenexa, Kans.: Addax Publishing Group, 1999.

Cameron, Steve. *George Brett: Last of a Breed.* Dallas: Taylor Publishing, 1993.

———. *Moments, Memories, Miracles: A Quarter Century with the Kansas City Royals.* Dallas: Taylor Publishing, 1992.

Carle, Bill. "Kansas City Royals: Building a Champion from Scratch in America's Heartland." In Peter C. Bjarkman, ed., *Encyclopedia of Major League Baseball: American League Team Histories.* Rev. ed. New York: Carroll and Graf Publishers, 1993, 183–204.

Dixon, Phil S. *The Ultimate Kansas City Baseball Trivia Quiz Book.* Shawnee, Kans.: Bon A Tirer, 1992.

Eskew, Alan. *A Royal Finish—The Celebration of the 1985 Kansas City Royals.* Chicago: Contemporary Books, 1985.

Garrity, John. *The George Brett Story.* New York: Coward, McCann and Geoghegan, 1981.

James, Bill. "Kansas City Royals—A History of Being a Kansas City Baseball Fan." In *The Bill James Baseball Abstract 1986.* New York: Ballantine Books, 1986, 39–71.

Kansas City Star. *George Brett: A Royal Hero.* Champaign, Ill.: Sports Publishing, 1999.

McCann, Mayer Hoffman. *The Economic Impact of the Kansas City Chiefs and the Kansas City Royals on the State of Missouri.* Kansas City: Mid-America Regional Council, 1989.

Martin, Mollie. *Kansas City Royals.* Mankato, Minn.: Creative Education Publishing Co., 1982.

Matthews, Denny. *Play by Play: 25 Years of Royals on Radio.* Lenexa, Kans.: Addax Publishing Group, 1999.

Morgan, Anne. *Prescription for Success: The Life and Values of Ewing Marion Kauffman.* Kansas City: Andrews and McMeel, 1995.

Rambeck, Richard. *The History of the Kansas City Royals.* Mankato, Minn.: Creative Education Publishing Co., 1999.

Rogan, Mike. *Kansas City Royals '93.* New York: Bantam Books, 1993.

Rothaus, James. *Kansas City Royals.* Mankato, Minn.: Creative Education Publishing Co., 1987.

Twyman, Gib. *Born to Hit: The George Brett Story.* New York: Random House, 1982.

Unions to Royals: The Story of Professional Baseball in Kansas City. Manhattan, Kans.: AG Press, 1996.

Zeeck, David, ed. *Number 5: George Brett and the Kansas City Royals.* Kansas City: Andrews and McMeel, 1993.

Zeligman, Mark, ed. *George Brett: A Royal Hero.* Champaign, Ill.: Sports Publishing, Inc., 1999.

St. Louis Browns

Beck, Peggy. "Working in the Shadows of Rickey and Robinson: Bill Veeck, Larry Doby and the Advancement of Black Players in Baseball." In Peter M. Rutkoff, ed., *The Cooperstown Symposium on Baseball and American Culture, 1997.* Jefferson, N.C.: McFarland and Co., 2000.

Borst, Bill. *Baseball through a Knothole: A St. Louis History.* St. Louis: Krank Press, 1980.

———. *The Best of Seasons: The 1944 St. Louis Cardinals and St. Louis Browns.* Jefferson, N.C.: McFarland and Co., 1995.

———. *Last in the American League: An Informal History of the St. Louis Browns.* St. Louis: Crank Press, 1978.

———. *Still Last in the American League: The St. Louis Browns Revisited.* West Bloomfield, Mich.: Altwerger and Mandel Publishing Co., 1992.

———, and Erv Fischer. *A Cornucopia of St. Louis Browns History and Trivia: A Jockstrap Full of Nails.* St. Louis: St. Louis Browns Historical Society, 1992.

Felber, Bill. "St. Louis Browns—Baltimore Orioles: One of the Very Worst, and One of the Very Best." In Peter C. Bjarkman, ed., *Encyclopedia of Major League Baseball: American League Team Histories.* Rev. ed. New York: Carroll and Graf Publishers, 1993, 358–89.

Godin, Roger A. *The 1922 St. Louis Browns: Best of the American League's Worst.* Jefferson, N.C.: McFarland and Co., 1991.

Goldstein, Richard. *Spartan Seasons: How Baseball Survived the Second World War.* New York: Macmillan, 1980.

Hawkins, John C. *This Date in Baltimore Orioles–St. Louis Browns History.* New York: Stein and Day, 1982.

Kashatus, William C. "A Season in the Sun: World War II Baseball, the 1945 St. Louis Browns, and a One-Armed Outfielder Named Gray." *Gateway Heritage* (summer 1991): 38–49.

———. *One-Armed Wonder: Pete Gray, Wartime Baseball, and the American Dream.* Jefferson, N.C.: McFarland and Co., 1995.

Leib, Frederick G. *The Baltimore Orioles: An Informal History of a Great Baseball Club in Baltimore and St. Louis.* New York: Putnam, 1955.

Mead, William B. *Baseball Goes to War: Stars Don Khaki, 4-Fs Vie for Pennant.* New York: Farragut Book Co., 1985. Original title, *Even the Browns.* Chicago: Contemporary Books, 1978.

Miller, James Edward. *The Baseball Business: Pursuing Pennants and Profits in Baltimore.* Chapel Hill: University of North Carolina Press, 1990.

Schiffer, Don. *My Greatest Baseball Game.* New York: A. S. Barnes and Co., 1950.

Smith, Gary N. "The St. Louis Browns." *Gateway Heritage* 4 (summer 1983): 8–15.

Van Lindt, Carson. *One Championship Season: The Story of the 1944 St. Louis Browns.* New York: Marabou Publishing, 1994.

Veeck, Bill, with Ed Linn. *The Hustler's Handbook.* New York: G. P. Putnam's Sons, 1965.

———. *Veeck, as in Wreck.* New York: G. P. Putnam's Sons, 1962.

Williams, Pat, and Michael Weinreb. *Marketing Your Dreams: Business and Life Lessons from Bill Veeck, Baseball's Marketing Genius.* Chicago: Sports Publishing, Inc., 2001.

St. Louis Cardinals

Alexander, Charles C. *Rogers Hornsby: A Biography.* New York: Henry Holt, 1995.

Anderson, Donald Ray. "Branch Rickey and the St. Louis Cardinals System: The Growth of an Idea." Ph.D. diss., University of Wisconsin, 1975.

Arndt, Rick. *Safe at Home: Ten Major League Baseball Players Discuss Their Careers and Their Christian Commitment.* St. Louis: Concordia Publishing House, 1979.

Broeg, Bob. *Bob Broeg's Redbirds: A Century of Cardinals' Baseball.* Marceline, Kans.: Walsworth Publishing Co., 1992.

———. *The Pilot Light and the Gashouse Gang: The Story of Frank Frisch and His Contemporaries.* St. Louis: Bethany Press, 1980.

———. "Reminiscences of Seasons Past." *Baseball History* 1, no. 3 (1986): 72–88.

———, and Jerry Vickery. *St. Louis Cardinals Encyclopedia.* Chicago: NTC/Contemporary Publishing Group, 1998.

Bowman, Larry G. "Christian Von der Ahe, the St. Louis Browns, and the World's Championship Playoffs, 1885–1888." *Missouri Historical Review* 91 (July 1997): 385–405.

Brown, Mary Louise. "The Stark and Anheuser-Busch Imagery, 1913–1933." *Gateway Heritage* 9 (fall 1988): 18–23.

Busch, August A., Jr. "Budweiser: A Century of Character." *Newcomen Society in North America* (January 6, 1955): 5–21.

Castle, George, and Jim Rygelski. *The I-55 Series: Cubs vs. Cardinals.* Champaign, Ill.: Sports Publishing, 1999.

Cepeda, Orlando, with Herb Fagan. *Baby Bull: From Hardball to Hard Time and Back.* Dallas: Taylor Publishing Co., 1998.

Craft, David, and Tom Owens. *Redbirds Revisited: Great Memories and Stories from St. Louis Cardinals.* Chicago: Bonus Books, 1990.

Davis, Jack E. "Baseball's Reluctant Challenge: Desegregating Major League Spring Training Sites, 1961–1964." *Journal of Sport History* 19 (summer 1992): 144–62.

Devaney, John. *The Greatest Cardinals of Them All.* New York: G. P. Putnam's Sons, 1968.

Egenriether, Richard. "Chris Von der Ahe: Baseball's Pioneering Huckster." *Baseball Research Journal* 18 (1989): 27–31.

Feldman, Doug. *Dizzy and the Gashouse Gang: The 1934 St. Louis Cardinals and Depression-Era Baseball.* Jefferson, N.C.: McFarland and Co., 2000.

Fleming, G. H. *The Dizziest Season: The Gashouse Gang Chases the Pennant.* New York: William Morrow and Co., 1984.

Flood, Curt, with Richard Carter. *The Way It Is.* New York: Trident Press, 1971.

Giglio, James N. *Musial: From Stash to Stan the Man.* Columbia: University of Missouri Press, 2001.

———. "Prelude to Greatness: Stanley Musial and the Springfield Cardinals of 1941." *Missouri Historical Review* 90 (July 1996): 429–52.

Gregory, Robert. *Diz: Dizzy Dean and Baseball during the Great Depression.* New York: Penguin Books, 1992.

Halberstam, David. *October 1964.* New York: Villard Books, 1994.

Hernon, Peter, and Terry Ganey. *Under the Influence: The Unauthorized Story of the Anheuser-Busch Dynasty.* New York: Simon and Schuster, 1991.

Herzog, Whitey, and Jonathan Pitts. *You're Missin' a Great Game: From Casey to Ozzie, the Magic of Baseball and How to Get it Back.* New York: Simon and Schuster, 1999.

Hetrick, J. Thomas. *Chris Von der Ahe and the St. Louis Browns.* Lanham, Md.: Scarecrow Press, 1999.

Hirshberg, Al. *Red Schoendienst: The Man Who Fought Back.* New York: Julian Messner, Inc., 1961.

———. *MISFITS! The Cleveland Spiders in 1899.* Jefferson, N.C.: McFarland, 1991.

Honig, Donald. *The St. Louis Cardinals: An Illustrated History.* New York: Prentice Hall, 1991.

Klein, Alan M. *Sugarball: The American Game, The Dominican Dream.* New Haven, Conn.: Yale University Press, 1991.

Konteleone, John J., ed. *Branch Rickey's Little Blue Book: Wit and Strategy from Baseball's Last Wise Man.* New York: Macmillan, 1995.

Lahsche, Jerry. *Stan the Man Musial: Born to Be a Ballplayer.* Dallas: Taylor Publishing Co., 1994.

Lieb, Fred. *The St. Louis Cardinals: The Story of a Great Baseball Team.* New York: G. P. Putnam's Sons, 1944.

Lipman, David. *Mr. Baseball: The Story of Branch Rickey.* New York: G. P. Putnam's Sons, 1966.

Murphy, B. Keith. "Curt Flood and Baseball's Reserve Clause: An Examination of Symbolic Martyrdom." *Journal of the Georgia Association of Historians* 18 (1997): 24–40.

Musial, Stan. *Stan Musial: "The Man's" Own Story, as Told to Bob Broeg.* Garden City, N.Y.: Doubleday and Co., 1964.

Rabinowitz, William Scott. "Thriving in Hard Times: The St. Louis Cardinals Make the Best of the Depression." *Gateway Heritage* 9, no. 1 (1988): 16–25.

Rains, Rob. *The St. Louis Cardinals: The 100th Anniversary History.* New York: St. Martins, 1992.

Ryan, Joan. "Flood's Fight Wasn't About the Money." *San Francisco Chronicle,* January 22, 1997.

Rygelski, Jim. "Baseball's 'Boss President': Chris Von der Ahe and the Nineteenth Century St. Louis Browns." *Gateway Heritage* (1992): 42–53.

Schiffer, Don, ed. *My Greatest Baseball Game.* New York: A. S. Barnes and Co., 1950.

Schoendienst, Red, with Rob Rains. *Red: A Baseball Life.* Champaign, Ill.: Sports Publishing, 1998.

Schoor, Gene. *The Red Schoendienst Story.* New York: G. P. Putnam's Sons, 1961.

Schulman, Henry. "Fight Ends for Flood." *San Francisco Examiner,* January 21, 1997.

Smith, Jeffrey E. "Jackie Robinson in Sportsman's Park." *Gateway Heritage* 17 (spring 1997): 50–53.

Staten, Vince. *Ol' Diz: A Biography of Dizzy Dean.* New York: HarperCollins, 1992.

Tiemann, Robert L. *Cardinal Classics: Outstanding Games from Each of the St. Louis Baseball Club's 100 Seasons, 1882–1981.* St. Louis: Baseball Histories, 1982.

Wright, Tina, ed. *Cardinal Memories: Recollections from Baseball's Greatest Fans.* Columbia: University of Missouri Press, 2000.

Index